Praise for *Employalty*

"The biggest leadership issue organizations face is creating a culture of committed team members in the new workplace. In *Employalty*, Joe Mull shows you how to attract and retain star employees that will help your company win in today's world."

JIM CLIFTON, Chairman of Gallup

"This is the book leaders have been looking for to stop turnover and staff shortages that plague their company! It has never been more important to learn how to create cultures, jobs, and career paths for employees that keep them engaged, and *Employalty* perfectly captures just that. Packed with expert advice and actionable steps, readers will walk away empowered to create better companies and teams."

DR. MARSHALL GOLDSMITH, *New York Times*–bestselling author of *What Got You Here Won't Get You There*

"Struggling to stay fully staffed? Read this book. Losing top talent to your competitors? Read this book. Baffled by what it takes to energize and engage employees today? Read. This. Book."

CY WAKEMAN, workplace drama researcher and *New York Times*–bestselling author of *No Ego*

"*Employalty* is a must-read. In it, Joe Mull shares his extraordinary experience catalyzing employee commitment. The lessons learned are tested and actionable. Get it, read it, but more importantly, put his suggestions into action."

DENISE HAMILTON, CEO and Founder, WatchHerWork

T0015331

"It's not easy to hire and retain top talent. That's why *Employalty* should be required reading for owners and executives of businesses, both large and small. Joe Mull provides a clear, simple framework for finding and keeping high-performing employees who will move your company forward."

DORIE CLARK, *Wall Street Journal*–bestselling author of *The Long Game* and executive education faculty at Duke University's Fuqua School of Business

"Work, the workforce, and the workplace are changing so rapidly that many books written about management and talent even a few years ago already feel out of date. Contrast that with Joe Mull's work in *Employalty*, which is forward-looking and full of timeless wisdom while practical and applicable for today. This is the rare perspective that rightly sees work as an ecosystem, with equal emphasis on being a great boss as to hiring and retaining top quality talent. Every manager and would-be manager, every leader at any level and of any stripe should read this book—as well as every person who wants to make the best moves for their career right now and in the years ahead."

KATE O'NEILL, Fortune 500 consultant and award-winning author of *Tech Humanist*

"Joe Mull smartly cracks the employee commitment code in a book that is engaging, clever, and personal. If your organization desires a humane, person-centered employee experience, *Employalty* is the path forward."

DAN PONTEFRACT, award-winning author of *Lead. Care. Win.* and *The Purpose Effect* and Thinkers50 Radar

EMPLOYALTY

EMPL

Joe Mull

OYALTY

How to Ignite Commitment
and Keep Top Talent
in the New Age of Work

Cataloguing in publication information is
available from Library and Archives Canada.
ISBN 978-1-77458-290-9 (paperback)
ISBN 978-1-77458-291-6 (ebook)
ISBN 978-1-77458-292-3 (audiobook)

Page Two
pagetwo.com

Edited by James Harbeck
Copyedited by Rachel Ironstone
Proofread by Alison Strobel
Cover design by Peter Cocking and Cameron McKague
Interior design and illustrations by Cameron McKague
Printed and bound in Canada by Friesens
Distributed in Canada by Raincoast Books
Distributed in the US and internationally by Macmillan

23 24 25 26 27   5 4 3 2 1

joemull.com

This book is for Lily, Miles, and Henry.
May you never settle for anything less than your Ideal Job,
doing Meaningful Work, for a Great Boss.

Contents

1 Where Does Commitment
Come From at Work? *1*

2 Becoming a
Destination Workplace *13*

3 The Breaking and
Upgrading of Work *35*

4 Rehumanization and the
Myth of Lazy *53*

IDEAL JOB

5 Compensation *73*

6 Workload *93*

7 Flexibility *111*

MEANINGFUL WORK

8 Purpose *131*

9 Strengths *149*

10 Belonging *165*

GREAT BOSS

11 Coaching *185*

12 Trust *201*

13 Advocacy *217*

14 Starting an Employalty Movement in Your Organization *235*

15 The Blockbuster Epilogue *251*

Acknowledgments *259*

Notes *263*

Where Does Commitment Come From at Work?

AS OFFICE BUILDINGS GO, the exterior of the Sun Building in Tulsa, Oklahoma, is... forgettable. At twelve stories high and with a sandstone and glass exterior, there is little to distinguish it to passersby. Its square shape gives the impression of a giant brown sugar cube, the size of a city block. It is surrounded by cracked parking lots and a smattering of small trees. For years, two bright Sunoco signs hung high atop the corners of the building, the only salute to its storied past, before they were removed in 2019. If you work in the Sun Building and your office is on the west side of the complex, a sprawling Home Depot invades your view.

Yet the building is a landmark.

"Everybody knows the Sun Building," says Joe Schrader. Joe has lived in Tulsa for thirty-five years and is the CEO of commercial lighting company Oklahoma LED. "It's not very sexy," he says, and laughs. "But for anyone in Tulsa, it's like, 'Oh yeah, I know where that is.'" Completed in 1954, the building originally housed the Sunray Oil Company, which eventually became part of Sunoco. In more recent decades, members of the community have visited the Sun Building to do banking, to attend conferences, to donate to blood drives, to get legal aid, to take tests, or to eat at the café inside. For almost seventy years, the building has been a daily presence in the lives of Tulsans. "It's an iconic building," Joe says.

He would know. Just five years after starting Oklahoma LED, his company was chosen to do a complete lighting conversion of the historic building. According to Joe, a full conversion is an involved project. "We change out every single light. If it's connected to electricity, we replace it. Hallways, offices, closets, cafeterias, restrooms, parking lots, all of it." When I ask him how such a young company scored such a high-profile contract, pride flashes across his face.

"We were the only company considered."

Joe Schrader founded Oklahoma LED in 2011. "I had read an article about LED lighting and that the industry would go from $50 million to $20 billion by 2020. I'd just sold my previous company and was looking for something as my next venture. I like to get out in front of trends and thought, *This is it.*" Remarkably, when Joe launched Oklahoma LED, he knew nothing about lighting and electricity. "By the way," he says, laughing, "if I ever start another business that I know nothing about, take me behind the woodshed and just punch me . . . as hard as you can. This is still one of the hardest things I've ever done."

But while Joe started a commercial lighting company with no knowledge of lighting, he did have clear ideas about how to treat the people he would hire. Having worked a variety of jobs throughout his career, Joe knew that feeling valued has a direct impact on how people show up.

"When I've been the hired help, I always appreciated how people treated me. If I'm a ditch digger, I want to work for a company that really values me as an employee, that doesn't treat me like just another number. Some days people have to freeze their butts off, or work in 105-degree weather, or come home at two in the morning because they're working second shift." Joe set out to create a competitive advantage for his company by how he treated the people who would work for him. He believed it would allow him to have the highest possible standards for who he hired and the quality of the work he expected. "My philosophy is, 'Take care of the people and people take care of the profits.' So, we pay higher than the market. They get four-day workweeks. We make sure everyone gets a vacation. We constantly tell them how much we appreciate them. We load 'em up with swag because we want them to be proud of our brand. These are real, tangible things they wouldn't get somewhere else. I just constantly ask, 'What can I do so that these employees think, *Man, they treat me so well here that I'd be a fool to go anywhere else?*"

Joe's philosophy has worked.

Oklahoma LED's turnover is minimal. They have their pick of electricians, laborers, and administrative staff. Their services consistently receive the highest possible customer ratings. Their reputation is so pristine, many of their largest contracts have been awarded without competing bids. Just a few years after they were founded, Oklahoma LED landed on *Inc.* magazine's list of the fastest growing privately held companies in America, where they stayed for three years. Joe's approach also allows him to have high standards. "My people are working really hard. They're traveling and working long days. That's why we treat them with so much respect. But we don't let people walk over us. We run a very tight ship. There are no skaters here. If you skate, you're gone." Asked if it's challenging to commit to pricier initiatives like higher pay, more time off, and employee gifts, he says no, there is a greater return: loyalty and production. In fact, he admits that his approach isn't entirely altruistic. "Greed has something to do with it. What I'm banking on is getting employees that give their all. That generosity is really reciprocity. I know that if I treat them well, I'm going to get loyalty in return. It's reciprocity, and it's an intended consequence."

That reciprocity is what has fueled Oklahoma LED's success. It's what made Oklahoma LED the clear choice to upgrade a local landmark like the Sun Building. That reciprocity is why Joe Schrader's company has minimal turnover, high engagement, a superior product, and year-over-year business growth.

That reciprocity—and the consistent results it produces—has a name:

It's called Employalty.

The Commitment Question

This book was born the moment I was stumped by a podcast interview question in 2021. After a robust thirty-minute conversation with the host about cultivating commitment at work—which I've studied and spoken about for nearly two decades—he moved to wrap up his show with one last question.

"Okay, Joe, let's put everything we just discussed into a nice, tidy package for those listening. In one sentence, where does commitment come from at work?"

I paused for what felt like an eternity. What came next was a word salad I'm not terribly proud of. "Well . . . I can't give it to you in one sentence," I said. "As we just talked about, it's, uh, complicated . . . there are a whole bunch of factors," which I then listed in a rambling brain dump.

I'm certain I sounded like the teacher from the old Charlie Brown cartoons I grew up with. Wah-wah-wah, wah-wah-wah-wah-wah . . .

My answer wasn't wrong. It just wasn't concise. That bothered me for weeks afterwards. We don't serve leaders or organizations well if we can't provide a clear, simple framework to nurture commitment among employees. How are folks like you supposed to do all the things it takes to get employees engaged if you first have to know and understand a lengthy list of *all* the things? You'd need to memorize a doctoral dissertation's worth of insight and actions to have any chance of getting it right. No wonder so many business owners, executives, and managers struggle to keep people motivated at work.

I became convinced: the world needs a one-sentence answer to the question "Where does commitment come from at work?" I set about the task of authoring that one sentence.

In the months following that podcast interview, I worked to synthesize my fifteen-plus years of studying commitment and training leaders with established and emerging research in what leads people at work to care and to try. It took a while, but I did it. After testing the ideas with my clients and audiences, I am certain that I've pinned down that one-sentence answer (you'll see it in a few moments). What I quickly realized, however, is that it would not be enough to answer just this one question. If you're like many of the leaders I work with, motivating employees isn't your only challenge. The other problem you're facing is getting people to join your organization in the first place.

The Future of Staffing

We are experiencing record-setting job switching and persistent staffing shortages across industries. There's a reason the phrase "the war for talent" exists. It's real and it's here.

Competition for both entry-level employees and experienced workers with more advanced education is fierce in the face of a triple-whammy. Fewer people are entering the labor force, more workers are leaving (to retire or start businesses), all while more and more jobs are being added to the economy. All three of these conditions are projected to continue for years. There simply aren't enough workers to fill all the jobs in the decade ahead. The biggest worker shortages are expected in healthcare, software, hospitality and leisure, management, and laborer positions.

Yet, numbers alone aren't the only challenge. There's another reason for so much job changing and understaffing across industries: a massive recalibration of how work fits into people's lives.

After years of increasing workloads, exploding schedules, demanding customers, stagnant pay, record burnout, and a global pandemic that took an already exhausted workforce and broke it, people have had enough. Workers are demanding less suffering at work. They want an end to the constant encroachment of their job into every aspect of their lives. They want more time, less stress, and better treatment. More than a decade of record-setting job changing across industries has made one thing clear: employees want a more humane employee experience.

And they're getting it.

In a competitive job market and across years of increased turnover, there are employers who *aren't* struggling to attract new workers or keep top talent. These businesses have their pick of the best talent available. Their employees stay, take on challenging work, maximize quality and effort, and as a result deliver outstanding products and services. What are these employers doing to avoid the staffing challenges that have hindered so many?

They have embraced a set of beliefs and behaviors that I have come to call *Employalty.*

The Employalty Effect

Employalty doesn't mean "employee loyalty." For too long that's been the expectation companies have had of anyone working under their logo: that upon hiring, employees will demonstrate unflinching loyalty in exchange for employment. Whether that's loyalty to a schedule, to quality, or to serve the mission of the organization, this has been the "deal" offered by employers for decades.

It's a deal that has been broken for much of that time.

No, Employalty is a portmanteau* of the words "employer," "loyalty," and "humanity." Employalty is the commitment employers make to consistently deliver a humane, person-centered employee experience, because that's what leads people to the highest levels of commitment at work. Yes, you can make the word "Employalty" from just "employer" and "loyalty," but you can't ignite commitment and retain talent in a post-Covid world—as I'll detail in the chapters ahead—without a more humane approach to the employee experience. So "humanity" is in there too.

Employalty is rooted in the idea that people *do* the best job possible when they believe they *have* the best job possible. It's not hard to find and keep devoted employees. Really, it's not. Treat them better than they would be treated elsewhere, and they'll join and stay. Create the conditions that activate their emotional and psychological commitment, and

---

* This is, without question, the fanciest word in this book. My eighth-grade English teacher would be so proud.

Employalty is rooted
in the idea that
people generally do
a great job when
they believe they *have*
a great job.

———————————

they'll care and try. When people join, stay, care, and try, every metric you pay attention to in your organization is positively impacted.

When you engineer the humane, person-centered employee experience detailed in this book, it sparks and sustains commitment. When employees' professional needs are met and their work is fulfilling, they take on challenges, navigate change, and do hard things. A committed workforce, in turn, produces a superior product or service. For committed employees, good isn't good enough; great becomes the standard. And when your team consistently does great work, everything you care about increases, including brand perception, reputation, sales, revenue, and growth.

Employalty also creates a competitive advantage in hiring. When the people who work for you describe your organization as the very best place to work, you attract a better caliber of candidate looking for *their* best place to work—and you also keep good people, so you lose less time and money replacing and retraining. The organizations you'll meet in this book understand the mindset required to effortlessly fill positions with top talent while rarely losing their rock-star employees.

There is no staffing shortage. There's a great jobs shortage.

Employalty is a clear, simple, evidence-based framework for finding great employees and igniting their commitment that will guide your organization now and into the future. Employalty is the path to better candidates, lower turnover, better service, superior quality, and outstanding performance. It's the recipe for happier employees *and* higher revenues. Imagine having a workforce that gives consistent energy and effort to their work every day. Imagine your employees being so engaged in what they do and who they do it for that they create a world-class customer experience every time. Imagine having minimal toxicity and drama on your teams because you've created an employee experience so special that individuals think and act carefully for fear of jeopardizing their place in it. Imagine knowing that a competitor will never be able to poach your best talent and that when the time comes to fill a position, you'll have your pick of the top talent from nearly anywhere.

It's all possible through Employalty.

What Lies Ahead

It turns out that this book answers not one, but three questions. It answers the commitment question: Where does commitment come from at work? It answers the staffing question: In this new age of work, how do we find and keep employees? And it answers the performance question: How do we take our company's performance to the next level?

The answer to all three is Employalty.

This is a book for business owners and executives who struggle to find and keep devoted employees. It's for those companies that want a more engaged workforce and a competitive advantage in hiring, quality, and performance. It's a book for leaders who want to make a case for changing how their organizations hire and treat employees. Because everything in this book is anchored in the research and trends of what most employees want out of a job, it's also a useful tool for job seekers and career changers to better understand the conditions to seek out for the highest degree of professional happiness.

In the pages ahead, you'll meet people and organizations from all types of industries: nonprofits, the trades, knowledge workers, and service industries, to name just a few, where the dimensions of Employalty are clearly influencing people and performance. As we explore their stories together, I'll tell you how to become a destination workplace, the kind people seek out, treasure, and rarely want to leave. I'll identify the exact conditions your company must create to sustain employee commitment and explain in detail how to install them in your organization. I'll share a plethora of research on why employees join, stay, care, and try... or don't. Along the way, I'll tell you why we're picking the wrong bosses, why the age of hiring is over, and why trying to find the best person for the job is an outdated strategy. I'll introduce you to the Employalty Scorecard, which will be your blueprint for activating commitment and retaining talent across your workforce. You will also get a set of tools to put the framework outlined in this book into action, turning ordinary people into devoted employees in your organization. There's even a downloadable resource kit that accompanies this book that you can get for free any time over at employaltybook.com.

Oh, and one more thing: I won't merely suggest what you must *do*. I'll outline what you must *believe* about how you treat employees who work for you. Because to achieve Employalty, you may have to adopt new values and beliefs about workers and challenge attitudes long held by others about people, employment, and work. Make no mistake, this is a book that advocates on behalf of employees for a better employee experience, not just because it's what's best for people, but also because it's what's best for business. The time has come for business owners and leaders in all industries to accept what Joe Schrader at Oklahoma LED and other leaders like him already know. Employalty isn't altruism. It's a business strategy. In this new era of work, it's the new cost of doing business well. It's the entry fee for success.

But let's start with the question that brought us here. Let's answer that podcast interviewer's query with the one sentence he sought and that took me nearly a year to finalize.

Because the answer is the foundation of the Employalty framework itself.

Where does commitment come from at work?

Commitment appears when people get to do their Ideal Job, doing Meaningful Work, for a Great Boss.

2

Becoming a
Destination Workplace

THE UNIVERSITY OF ALABAMA has the top college football program in the US. The Crimson Tide, as they are known, have dominated college football for fourteen years and counting. Since 2009, they have played for nine national championships, winning six titles. They played in six of the first seven College Football Playoff national title tournaments, which began in 2014. In the 180 weekly Associated Press ranking polls released between the end of the 2010 season and the end of the 2021 season—that's twelve years of college football ranking polls—they were ranked outside of the top ten for a total of... two weeks.

And Alabama doesn't just beat their opponents. They annihilate them.

In College Football Playoff games—the tournament that pits the nation's top four teams each season against each other to determine a champion—Alabama's margin of victory in recent games has been by 38, 17, 18, 11, 17, and 21 points.

Alabama fans' rallying cry is "Roll Tide," and they have. They've rolled over every other college football program in the US for nearly two decades, creating the greatest dynasty the storied history of the sport has ever seen. In the world of college football, there is Alabama, and there is everyone else.

You don't need to be a sports fan, or even like sports, to learn from this kind of success. The college football program at the University of Alabama has a lot to teach us about recruiting top talent, developing them, and then benefiting greatly from their contributions. What they've been doing for fourteen-plus years is what companies like yours need to start doing now to find the best people and inspire them to give their very best to your organization.

Alabama's approach isn't a secret. They maintain an institutional commitment to excelling at football at the highest level. They prioritize being the best. They recruit the best athletes, provide the best facilities, hire the best coaches, and deliver the best experience for players. This is both their method and their mantra. If you want a chance at a career in pro football, you want to go to Alabama. If you are being recruited by Alabama, it's a signal that you are among the best young players in the world.

Lots of other schools have made similar attempts at greatness. Hundreds of millions of dollars have been spent by colleges large and small to duplicate Alabama's success. Many programs have targeted elite players, invested in high-end facilities, and lured a big-name coach to their school. While some have enjoyed flashes of triumph, none has sustained the kind of success that Alabama has, and that is because Alabama has done one thing consistently that most other programs haven't.

Alabama delivers on the promises they make to their players.

When prized student athletes are weighing where to enroll, they know they are entering into a mutually beneficial transaction with a program. The student athlete will devote their time, focus, effort, and talent to the team. In exchange, the student wants to go to the place that gives them the best chance to fulfill their personal and professional dreams. Alabama's football recruiters know this and build their entire recruiting pitch on their program being the best way for the recruit to get where he wants to go. We can imagine what those conversations sound like:

> Dream of playing in the NFL? We currently have fifty-three alumni in the league, more than any other program.

> Want to become great at your position? Let me introduce you to your position coach, who is one of the best in the country.

> Want to win a championship? Every recruiting class in the last sixteen years has won a title. Every. Single. One.*

All football programs do this. As soon as recruiters identify worthy talent, they work to convince the player that their organization is their best chance at achieving their dreams. They highlight their facilities, support services, the other talent in the organization, and the leaders and coaches committed to the player's success. Where the school has a proven track record of accomplishment, it's put on full display. Where a program lacks that history, they sell hope and the chance to be a part of something great that's just around the corner. Once the recruit decides that the program is the right fit for them, they commit. Together, the student and the program go about the work of achieving their shared goals.

---

* This stat is just bananas. Alabama coaches have told thousands of kids over the years, "Join our team, and you'll win a championship," and it's *never* not been true. Since 2006, every kid who has heard it, enrolled, and stayed three years has won a title. That's nuts.

Where schools deliver on their promises to recruits, they enjoy deep commitment from elite talent who perform at the highest level. For the programs that fail to provide the experience sought by players, that commitment disappears.

This is *literally* true. If at any point the program stops meeting the wants and needs of the recruit, they can de-commit from the program. Unhappy players can initiate a transfer to a new school, one that gives them what they're not getting at their current one.*

This is the world we're in right now when it comes to finding and keeping devoted employees. If you want to attract and keep the best people, they need to believe yours is the job that best meets all their wants and needs. This may require you to change your mindset about how you fill positions at your company. Stop hiring. Get out of a selection mindset. We now live in the age of recruiting. You don't get to pick people; you must attract them to your organization. The era of trying to find the best person for the job is over. You must now create the best *job* for the *person*. In this way, you have to start thinking and acting like a college football recruiter.

You're a single parent with young kids at home? We offer flexible schedules, remote work, and a bank of PTO (paid time off) to draw from on day one.

Want to gain more experience and enhance your skills in a specific area? We have a thriving mentorship program, and you'll spend at least five hours a month with your mentor.

---

* College football isn't perfect. An argument can be made that it exploits young people in the name of producing ungodly sums of money for universities, coaches, and media. A disproportionate number of these young people are Black and poor. This is all true as well.

Need to earn more? Our pay scales are in the top 5 percent of the market. We pride ourselves on paying at the top of industry scales.

Corporate recruiters have been operating this way for years for hard-to-fill positions where the supply of candidates regularly falls short of demand. They sell how their company allows the employee to live the life they want to live. These recruiters understand that in a competitive market, they don't get to pick the talent. The talent has to pick them. And in an environment where nearly all workers have become more selective of where and how they work, this approach is required to fill nearly all positions. Whether they have a need for restaurant employees, call center workers, or skilled trades, employers don't get to pick the talent anymore.

They have to pick you.

Like Alabama did with football, your company must establish and maintain an institutional commitment to a humane, person-centered employee experience across your organization. This needs to be both your method and your mantra. But here's the good news: we know what employees are looking for. Despite wildly different labels, assessments, and findings, nearly every piece of research published in the last twenty years on attracting, keeping, and inspiring employees has pointed again, and again, and again to three primary factors.

The Three Factors of Employalty

Where does commitment at work come from? What leads someone to join a team, put forth maximum effort on the job, care deeply about the work, and stay with an organization over time? I've spent the better part of fifteen years answering this question. My answer reflects a wide-ranging body of social science and organizational development research, my own work studying commitment and helping leaders create engagement on teams across the US, and a mountain of anecdotal evidence from leaders and workers alike. Being able to clearly articulate where commitment in the workplace comes from in a simple and evidence-based way has been my life's work to date. And so I present to you now, dear reader, the culmination of that work and what is, in my estimation, the single most important sentence in this book:

Commitment appears when employees get to do their Ideal Job, doing Meaningful Work, for a Great Boss.

These three concepts—which I will call "factors" throughout this book—provide the blueprint to getting employees to join, stay, care, and try. They are the recipe for turning your organization into a destination workplace. When each employee working for you enjoys their Ideal Job, doing Meaningful Work, for a Great Boss, the benefits to your organization are many.

Let's briefly examine these factors one at a time.

Ideal Job: The first factor is what I get, as an employee, in exchange for my employment. Do the nuts and bolts of the job— the financials, schedule, workload, and work arrangement— fit into my life in an ideal way? At a time when so many have prioritized working to live over living to work, a job has become one puzzle piece in a larger picture. When it snaps into place perfectly, bringing the rest of the image to life, commitment gains energy. Though every person is different and there are numerous ingredients to a role being someone's Ideal Job, there are three dimensions to the Ideal Job factor: compensation, workload, and flexibility.

Meaningful Work: The second factor is what employees experience in the course of doing their work, day in and day out. A nearly endless parade of research over the last three decades has made it clear that there are a handful of experiences employees must have in their work that have a direct influence on commitment. For example, we know that believing in the mission or purpose of a company holds tremendous sway over employee commitment. So, too, does believing that our individual contributions are valued, as does taking on work that unleashes our unique gifts and creativity. To compartmentalize many of these findings into something easy to translate, I've identified three dimensions to the Meaningful Work factor: purpose, strengths, and belonging.

Great Boss: The third factor is the person or persons responsible for overseeing an employee's day-to-day work. Direct supervisors are the single most influential factor in the employee experience. Years of research suggest that bosses are the biggest reason someone leaves a job or stays. If an employee consistently has a psychologically fulfilling experience in the workplace, it's because their boss helps facilitate it. In fact, Gallup found that the team leader alone accounts for 70 percent of the variance in a team's engagement. Make no mistake: commitment comes from better bosses. And there are dozens (and dozens and dozens) of things a leader must do well to be a Great Boss. Genuinely caring about each employee as a person and about their career path is crucial. So are competence, visibility, support, humility, approachability, vulnerability... Once again, to create a digestible, usable model, I've distilled these dynamics into three dimensions. To earn the label of Great Boss,* a leader must engage in coaching, trust, and advocacy.

---

* For the record, I don't treat the word "boss" like a dirty word because it's a word people use conversationally. (If you ask your neighbor what they think of their new boss, they're not going to be offended by the word.) Instead of spending our energy on debates like whether the word "leader" is good, and "boss" is bad, let's instead put that energy toward making sure we don't show up in the world as a bad boss.

Each of these nine dimensions that make up our three factors will be the focus of its own chapter. But the first thing to understand is that these three factors—Ideal Job, Meaningful Work, and Great Boss—work together to create a destination workplace. When they are each consistently present in the employee experience, commitment appears. That commitment, in turn and across a team, produces a multitude of desired business results, including retention, reputation, and revenue.

I've found that the best way to illustrate these concepts—how they work together and the commitment they cultivate when all three are present—is with a Venn diagram. In its simplest form, our model has a "C" for commitment at its center, where the three factors converge:

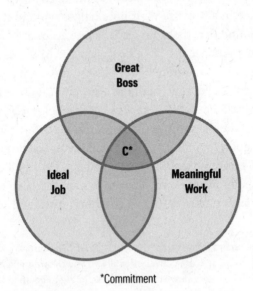

*Commitment

When I or a member of my team teach this model to leaders at retreats or during conference keynotes, we always add the three dimensions of each factor in the diagram as a way to completely represent what we must engineer for employees at work.

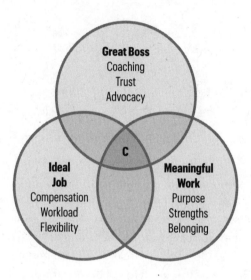

When walking leaders through this model, we also include the specific results that companies experience when these factors are present. We showcase how these three factors impact retention, reputation, and revenue, as well as the codependencies that exist to produce these results. You can see that overlap in the next iteration of our Venn diagram.

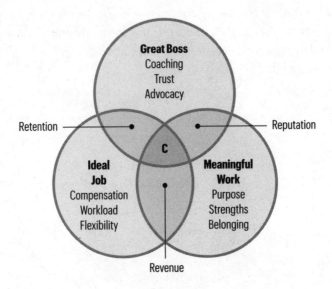

What's powerful about using this illustration is that it helps us see how some results are both produced by and dependent on adjacent factors. For example, when employees get their Ideal Job and a Great Boss, the company experiences *retention*. After all, when workers are paid well, have a manageable workload, and enjoy flexibility *and* they have a great leader, they typically don't leave. This is often true even if they don't have Meaningful Work. The downside to employee retention without fulfilling work is that, at times, quality suffers. So both revenue and reputation are negatively affected.

On the other side of our model, when employees experience Meaningful Work and a Great Boss, they tell others. This positively impacts *reputation*. That company will attract talent. Workers say to friends and family, "You should get

Commitment appears
when employees get
to do their Ideal Job,
doing Meaningful Work,
for a Great Boss.

_____

a job at my company. The work is really satisfying, and our boss is great." They say this even when some or all aspects of the Ideal Job aren't present (for example, when the company doesn't pay at the top of the market). That reputation extends to clients as well. The market sees quality and responds with interest. When an Ideal Job is absent, though, you often see long-term retention struggles. Your top talent can be lured elsewhere with higher wages, a more manageable workload, or more flexibility in when, where, and how they work. And if you're experiencing turnover, that negatively impacts revenue.

And in the case of an organization that provides an Ideal Job doing Meaningful Work but whose employees suffer under a not-great boss, there will still be *revenue*, but workers won't testify about the company to others (no reputation) and will eventually leave (no retention).

In other words, it takes all three factors, working together, to create a destination workplace that cultivates commitment and produces the business results of retention, reputation, and revenue.

Nearly every story you've ever heard about someone leaving a job can be attributed to Ideal Job, Meaningful Work, and Great Boss. Drill down on the details of those stories, and you'll discern the nine dimensions within those three factors. The same is true with every story you've heard about why someone chooses to take a new job or stay with an organization. Likewise, nearly every piece of credible research on staffing turnover and employee engagement released in recent years, in one way or another, highlights one or more of these dimensions as the contributing or significant factor.

This model is the blueprint for Employalty and turning your organization into a destination workplace. When your organization ensures that each employee gets their Ideal Job doing Meaningful Work for a Great Boss, you are essentially formulating commitment across your workforce. Employalty becomes your competitive advantage. But this model doesn't just serve as an organizational road map for increasing commitment, and with it retention, reputation, and revenue. It also allows you to create an Employalty Scorecard for every individual in your organization. To show you what I mean, let's examine these factors and their dimensions against the employee experience of a devoted worker who recently changed jobs.

The Caregiver

Paige McMullen knew it was time to start job searching when her boss wrote her up on her wedding day.

Paige was the Activity Director in the memory care unit of a lavish assisted living community in eastern Ohio. This was her first job out of college, and for much of her time in it, she felt like a failure. "I spent a lot of time thinking the problem was me. That's definitely part of what kept me there for a while," she told me.

Anyone who works in senior care knows that it takes a special breed of person to make it their career. For many, including Paige, it's a calling. "I always knew I wanted to work with seniors. I don't know how to explain it. It's like... I get to give back to people who have given their lives to something else along the way. I get to brighten their day or provide comfort or help them manage things. It just feels like the most meaningful way to be of service."

Nobody goes into a career in senior care for the money. Sadly, caregiver professions are among the most demanding yet underpaid careers anywhere. That's why, despite having graduated from a liberal arts college with a four-year degree in recreational therapy and taking a role supervising three to five activity aides, Paige's starting wage as Activity Director was $13.25 an hour. She was also expected to work every other holiday and weekend. "Would I have liked to make more? Sure. But it wasn't about the money," she says. "Low pay, working weekends and holidays... that's just how it is in long-term care."

In the early months of her new job, Paige struggled with her new boss's style. "Our interactions were limited strictly to what she wanted me to do. She'd say, 'I expect you spend X hours on the floor with residents, lead X number of activities a week, do all this paperwork and these reports, and track the work of these three aides.' Otherwise, she didn't talk to me. There was no personal interaction. This is a job that takes a ton of personal energy, compassion, and focus, and I didn't have a lot of manager training, so I always felt like I was learning on the fly. I needed support. I needed a mentor. But she was cold. She stayed in her office all the time. She was never encouraging. I can count on one hand the number of times I got a compliment from her." If this sounds like sour grapes from someone who just didn't gel with their boss's style, it's not. "Across the unit, aides, transporters, dietary, administration, everyone struggled with her. Believe me, the team notices when there's a leader who isn't encouraging, never leaves her office, and never lends a hand with care or transport."

In addition to having no support from her boss, Paige struggled with the workload. "I was planning events, buying supplies, supervising aides, leading groups, scheduling entertainers, assisting with residents, running family support groups, doing a dozen reports or spreadsheets a month... it was overwhelming. I always had to stay late, and I always felt behind."

Fresh out of school, she kept thinking her struggles were about her inexperience. "I thought there was something wrong with me. I went in every day and gave everything I could. It took me a long time to accept that I wasn't the problem. It wasn't until I heard that the unit had previously employed two Activity Directors and that they had downsized to one, me, that I started to think, *Okay, their expectations of what one person can reasonably accomplish here are way off.*" But Paige kept at it. "I valued the mission of the company. I liked their approach to families and their holistic caregiving approach. I believed in that. I also liked my colleagues. I felt a loyalty to the company and my team."

Knowing what you know about the three factors that create a destination workplace, Paige's scorecard might look something like this:

Paige McMullen's Employalty Scorecard

GB
× Coaching
× Trust
× Advocacy

C

IJ
× Compensation
× Workload
× Flexibility

MW
✓ Purpose
✓ Strengths
✓ Belonging

In her job Paige was only experiencing Meaningful Work. Her boss was giving her none of what she needed to nurture her commitment, and the circumstances of her role—pay, workload, job flexibility—were lacking. For any employee missing two out of three of these factors, it's only a matter of time until they stop caring about the work, or leave, or both.

Though Paige never stopped caring, she did eventually leave. After two years in the job, things came to a head for Paige the week she got married. She stopped by the unit to check her mailbox on the day between her wedding and honeymoon. Inside was a disciplinary write-up from her boss. It was dated the day of Paige's wedding. While she was out, it was discovered that a date had been listed incorrectly on a flyer for a family support group meeting. Her boss wrote her up for failing to perform the duties of her job. Paige was floored. "Yes, it shouldn't have happened. I'll make no excuse about that. But the write-up, the lack of a conversation, the lack of any kind of grace while working in that demanding role and getting married, it bothered me. Especially when I'd never been written up or even talked to about any kind of performance issue previously." A few weeks later, Paige resigned. She found a new role at a senior care facility closer to home.

Her new job was night-and-day different from her old one.

"The first thing I noticed about the administrator was how warm and personable he was to everyone in the building. That was a breath of fresh air. But the main reason I took the job was the amount of creative freedom I was going to have to help launch a specialty unit in the building." Paige's new title is Memory Care Coordinator. From the moment she applied for the job, her new boss, Ryan, loved her rec therapy background and the additional dimension it brought to the new memory care unit they were opening on campus. Paige laughs thinking back. "It didn't even feel like a job interview.

We ended up excitedly tossing around ideas of all the innovative things we could do with the new wing they were starting from scratch." When Ryan offered her the job at $18.50 an hour, she couldn't say yes fast enough. "The extra money wasn't the reason I took the job. It's a nice bonus. It's nice to have a tiny bit of financial breathing room. But I'm here because I love what we do and how we do it. I have a boss who is supportive, who wants ideas and updates, but who lets me handle things the best way I see fit."

The other big change is how her new boss operates day to day.

"He isn't above doing anything. When we're short-staffed, he helps get residents dressed and fed. He spends time on the floor. I've even seen him changing briefs. You can't imagine what that says to everyone else on the team. My brain ties it to our worth. What we do every day is really important. When he's not above any of that, it's an acknowledgment of how valuable we are."

Paige says she can't imagine leaving her new employer. "I feel really lucky. I know that not everyone feels like they're paid well and treated well while getting to do work they love. I know I'm fortunate in that way. No, I don't plan on going anywhere for a long time."

After one year in her new job, Paige's Employalty Scorecard is full of check marks.

Paige McMullen's New Job Employalty Scorecard

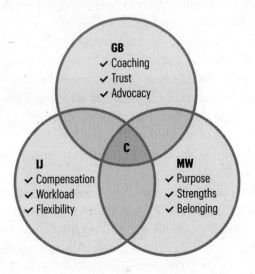

Will Paige stay in this job forever? That's the wrong question. The better question is, *What would cause a devoted employee like Paige to leave or become disengaged?* What I know for certain is that if circumstances around her change, and those changes result in some of these elements being taken away, Paige will notice it quickly. When anyone finds themselves in a role where all three of the Employalty elements are present, and then some aspect of that experience slips or deteriorates, commitment is jeopardized. For example, what happens if Ryan moves on from Paige's company? If Paige's new boss doesn't show her the same confidence and support that she enjoys under Ryan's supervision, her commitment could wane. Suddenly she'd find herself experiencing only two of the three elements of Employalty. That single change in leadership—the exodus of one influential person—could transform her employer from a destination workplace to a departure organization, for Paige and for others who work there.

The other dynamic at play here involves the unique values, beliefs, and desires of each individual employee. As Paige herself indicated, some factors are more important to her than others. Clearly, Meaningful Work ranks higher than any other factor when it comes to Paige's emotional and psychological commitment. Taking her priorities into consideration, a more accurate depiction of her Employalty Scorecard would place greater emphasis on these values and preferences. In her case, it should look like this:

Paige McMullen's Adjusted Employalty Scorecard

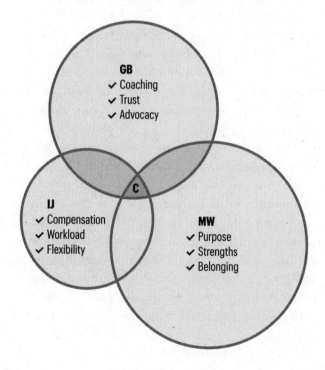

What's critical to understand is that Paige's scorecard will not look like this forever. This illustration is simply a reflection of where she is in her career at this time. What happens if, say three years from now, Paige becomes a mother? With a child at home, it is likely that there would be shifts in what she needs and wants from her job. At a minimum, it's probably safe to assume that the size of that Ideal Job circle would increase as she requires a more manageable workload and greater flexibility in when and how she works. At the same time, the other areas of Meaningful Work and Great Boss won't necessarily become *less* important. If or when a change like that unfolds in Paige's life, it will be her employer's ability to adapt to her changing needs that will determine whether the company will be able to retain her and whether she will continue to experience emotional and psychological commitment. Interestingly, it will be her supervisor's ability to read and react to these changes that will (or will not) contribute to Paige's perception of her supervisor as a Great Boss, even if that factor of Employalty takes on lesser significance to Paige.

As we work to create destination workplaces, we must understand that while commitment isn't fleeting, it is both fragile and variable. Each person in your organization has their own internal scorecard. What is checked on one person's may be lacking on another's. Also, priorities differ from person to person, and each person's priorities change over the course of their lives for many reasons. Commitment is subject to a complex mix of conditions and seasons, like plants in a flowerbed. You can get many things right with your gardening—fertilizer, sunlight, spacing, pruning—but if the plants don't get enough water, not only will they fail to thrive, eventually, they'll die out. Likewise, when even one small piece of the total employee experience necessary is lacking, commitment is at risk.*

This fragility is why your company's commitment to Employalty is so important. Use the three factors outlined here—Ideal Job, Meaningful Work, and Great Boss—as the road map by which you drive organizational values and decisions, and you'll position your organization to reap all the rewards of Employalty. You'll enjoy a competitive advantage in hiring while simultaneously being able to become more selective about who you hire. The people who join will care, try, and stay. They'll do quality work, even when it's hard, driving reputation and revenue.

In coming chapters, I'll show you how to deliver Ideal Job, Meaningful Work, and Great Boss for each of the people on your team so you can reap all the joys and benefits of a committed workforce. But first, we must understand how we got to this place. Leaders and business owners have been building departure organizations for years, they just didn't know it. Before we can create a destination workplace, we must understand exactly what's been broken for so long—and why—and what can be done about it.

---

* We've provided a blank Employalty Scorecard in the digital toolkit that accompanies this book. Just visit employaltybook.com to download it.

3

The Breaking and Upgrading of Work

WHAT I'LL remember the most is when the doctor began to cry.

A few months into the Covid-19 pandemic, I was invited to be the keynote speaker at a virtual all-company meeting for a multisite urgent care group in Colorado. Management had organized the event as a way to show the staff their appreciation and to help them process all they were facing as the Covid-19 global pandemic dragged on.

The way their work lives had changed was astonishing.

The meeting kicked off with a review of their current patient traffic. Prior to the start of the pandemic, they averaged 585 appointments a day across their enterprise. On the day of our meeting, they were averaging 14,043. In the early months of the pandemic, they averaged 2,800 calls a day. By the fall, that number had soared to 12,000. To call this change in volume unprecedented would be an understatement. Team members explained that the phone literally never stopped ringing. At no time could a staff member pick up the phone and get a dial tone. If they lifted the receiver, they were answering a call. At the time of our program, administrators were still trying to come up with a way for employees to make calls out of their sites.

For eight months, these employees had been running mobile Covid-19 testing sites. On an average day, employees swabbed four hundred runny noses while standing outside in a parking lot for twelve hours, covered head to toe in protective equipment. Then they'd do it again the next day. And the next. And the next. When they reviewed these numbers in the virtual event, nobody complained. In fact, their responses were the opposite of self-pity. Their comments in the chat box revealed their commitment and their character.

It needs to be done.

We're saving lives.

It kills me when kids test positive.

When it was his turn to speak, the lead physician—an experienced, battle-tested doctor in his early sixties—choked back tears. A combination of exhaustion, frustration, and extraordinary pride poured out. He told his employees how proud he was to know each of them. He swore up and down that they were going to get through this. He promised to do whatever it took to help them keep going. He implored them not to give a second of their attention to the absurd fools who would downplay the crisis. He rightly proclaimed that when the dust settled, there would be an innumerable mass who owed their lives to these people. His comments were heartfelt, and his staff needed to hear them.* Though many described the event as helpful, it was obvious that the preceding months had taken a toll.

They didn't know at the time that the pandemic would continue for another two years.

In the months following our virtual event, this committed group of healthcare professionals changed. In the face of exhaustion, constant risk of infection, and the everlasting crush of repetitive, daily work, the meaning and fulfillment they felt during the first months of the pandemic slowly evaporated. Some team members quit. Others kept going to work but admitted to being "zombies" who were just going through the motions. Many described becoming cold and resentful toward members of their community who refused to take action, like masking and getting the vaccine when it became available, to stop the spread of the virus.

This happened to teams everywhere.

Those who study the impact of stress on the body say that the collective trauma of the relentless Covid-19 pandemic delivered both chronic and acute stressors to people from nearly all walks of life, taxing our hearts, muscles, immune systems, and central nervous systems. Just a few months into the pandemic, mental health professionals reported seeing a threefold increase in depression, a 30 percent increase in anxiety, and frightening increases in eating disorders and substance abuse. Indeed, emerging research is only just now shining a light on the corrosive impact the pandemic had on subsets of our population including children, college students, healthcare workers, teachers, counselors, and parents. More than two years of data suggest a devastating effect, one with a long tail, on nearly every area of our lives. There is one

---

* His remarks to his team were deeply moving and far more powerful than anything I, the "professional speaker," could have said. It's a reminder to all leaders to be vulnerable, speak from the heart, and be generous with gratitude.

consequence, however, that emerged as more prevalent than any other. It's what happened to countless professionals in workplaces the world over. It's precisely what happened to the team at the overrun urgent care clinics in Colorado.

Burnout.

The World Health Organization defines burnout as a syndrome resulting from "chronic workplace stress that has not been successfully managed." It is characterized by factors including exhaustion, increased mental distance from one's job, feelings of negativity or cynicism, and reduced effectiveness. The spread of burnout during the Covid-19 crisis was staggering. A whopping 77 percent of employees reported feeling burned out just months into the pandemic. When workplaces began bringing employees back to offices, 72 percent of those returning who had been working virtually reported feeling burned out. That's higher than workers who kept going to work during the pandemic (60 percent) and more than those who kept a hybrid schedule (65 percent).* At the end of 2021, three out of five workers reported negative impacts of work-related stress, including lack of interest, motivation, energy, and effort at work. Meanwhile, one in three workers reported cognitive weariness and emotional exhaustion, and nearly half of all workers reported physical fatigue—a 38 percent increase across the workforce in less than twenty-four months. A few months later, the American Psychological Association proclaimed that burnout had become "persistent and indefinite." Burnout and exhaustion extended in every direction.

It should come as no surprise, then, that many point to the Covid-19 pandemic as the cause of spikes in burnout and a mass exodus of workers across industries. After all, it is

---

* So, if you think the folks who worked from home full-time somehow had it easier, they didn't.

reasonable to suggest that a years-long traumatic event that impacted every country in the world would be the cause of so much exhaustion and turnover. But it's not true. The unprecedented levels of burnout and exhaustion experienced by workers, and the staffing crisis that followed, were not caused by the Covid-19 pandemic.

The real cause began more than forty years ago.

The Rise and Rise and Rise of Work

She lingered at the end of the line of people waiting to chat with me after my keynote program. She wasn't really *in* the line. She was drifting along the back wall, eyes downcast, periodically glancing up. I'd seen this before. I knew she was waiting for the room to empty.

I had just stepped off the stage at a large ophthalmology conference in Las Vegas. This was one of the first in-person speaking events I had taken in eighteen months. I had just finished delivering a keynote presentation on what it would take to re-energize teams after more than a year of the pandemic. During the session, I forcefully debunked some of the myths floating around that the recent flood of resignations was due to a decline in work ethic. With the room nearly deserted, she made her way over. When she reached me, she spoke almost in a whisper.

"I have to tell you... what you just said..."

Then... she started to cry. Gathering herself quickly, she took a breath and started again.

"I have to tell you that what you just said... I just really needed to hear it."

Her name was Joyce, and she went on to tell me that she had recently resigned from her position as a Practice Administrator for a large physician group after seventeen years. She described being the primary person running the business for nearly two decades.

"I was proud to do whatever it took to take care of my doctors."

As the company grew, so did her workload. In addition to supervising all the employees at multiple locations, Joyce managed schedules, reporting, and payroll. She was the point person for hiring, training, and team cohesion issues. She was known to rotate to different offices, covering shifts and pitching in wherever needed. Year after year, she had more people to manage, more duties on her plate, and more fires to put out.

Long after her demanding role passed the point of being reasonable for one person to sustain, she started asking for help. "I told the partners that we needed to hire at least one other manager. I told them I couldn't keep going like this. They kept saying they believed I could handle it. The truth is, they didn't want to spend the money." As years passed, Joyce continued asking for help. Eventually, she begged. At one point, she offered to forgo raises. In another conversation, she offered to cut her own salary to make room for a second manager. But no help came.

When the pandemic arrived, her situation went from awful to impossible. After agonizing over the decision, Joyce quit. She stifled sobs as she told me her story. "I got my doctors through lawsuits, regulatory changes, and financial distress. I kept their livelihoods intact again and again. And do you know that when I went in to resign after seventeen years of doing everything for them, even when it took a toll on my health and my family, do you know what they said?"

Her anger was palpable. She could barely get the words out.

"They questioned my work ethic."

For anyone reading this book, Joyce's story is probably familiar. I'd bet that you can think of a time in recent years when the amount of work you were expected to handle in your job far exceeded what was reasonable for one person. I'd also bet that this increase wasn't limited to a single project or busy season. Rather, it's more likely that your burden has increased incrementally over the years, with your workload ultimately reaching (or exceeding) your max capacity some time ago, and it's stayed there. Joyce's experience is not an isolated one. Decades of data prove how workloads and work hours have continued to swell.

In Australia, a nationally representative poll found that the average worker logs more than six hours of additional unpaid work every week. This is up from five in 2020, and just over four in 2019. That's 312 hours a year, essentially adding *eight weeks* of additional *unpaid* labor to an employee's calendar. Workers are doing more work every year, and they aren't being paid for it. In the UK, British workers toil for nearly two hours a week more than the EU average, equivalent to an extra two and a half weeks a year. One study found that 91 percent of white-collar office professionals in the UK are working beyond their weekly contracted hours, with the majority admitting they do it because they feel pressured by their workload. Of those who work beyond their contracted hours, 90 percent receive no form of additional compensation.

Yet it is the US that claims the title as the most over-worked industrialized nation on earth.

In research conducted *prior to* the Covid pandemic, 76 percent of Americans reported working more than forty-six hours a week. Americans work hundreds of hours a year more than the citizens of other G7 nations, including 137 hours a year more than the Japanese, 260 hours a year more than the British, and 499 hours a year more than the French. One reason for this disparity might be that the US doesn't have a law limiting the length of the workweek.*

---

* There are 134 countries on earth that have laws limiting the length of the workweek. The US is not one of them.

Work hours in the US aren't the only devastating disparity. As workloads for Americans have increased, time away from work has dwindled. An examination of vacation time offered to American workers compared to the rest of the developed world reveals that we don't get as much, and we don't use what we do get. In nearly every other industrialized nation on earth, the average worker gets twenty paid vacation days a year. In Finland and France, it's thirty. In the US, the average worker gets just over nine paid days of vacation per year. But that doesn't really tell the story. This is the bigger travesty:

One in four American workers get no paid vacation days.

Despite this pittance by comparison, only 44 percent of American workers use all their vacation time each year. In fact, the number of vacation days taken by the average American in a year has dropped by 20 percent since 1981, with the most significant drop taking place at the turn of the millennium. If Americans vacationed as they did before 2000, it would equate to 447 million additional days of vacation time being used in the US. Employees list several reasons for not using their allotted time off. Some workers forgo vacations because their PTO banks must also be used for sick time or childcare issues, forcing workers to save time for anticipated medical needs or "just in case." For some employees, a lack of discretionary income makes taking a vacation an out-of-reach luxury. Others point to a workplace culture where vacations are discouraged by management or feared by some workers as a signal of lesser dedication. But the most cited reason among Americans for not taking vacation time?

Fear of falling behind at work.

Over decades, what takes up time and space in our lives as "work" has grown exponentially. In some workplaces, cutbacks, reductions, and "right-sizing" took what was once the work of two to three people and foisted it onto an individual. Managers especially bore the brunt of this workload expansion. In just the last ten years, the number of direct reports per manager increased by 30 percent in the US. In some places, demanding leaders used promises of wealth and fear of job loss to drive ambitious workers into a cult of overworking. Combined with the diminishing power and presence of unions to protect workers and the intense lobbying of political parties by businesses to avoid legislating more stringent worker protections, these conditions have led to years of increasing, expanding, unending work. Slowly but steadily, one decade after another, the volume of work expected from employees in nearly every industry has increased. Simultaneously, our time away from work to recover and recharge has decreased. And like the frog who was placed in the pot of cold water on the stove then had the heat turned up, we didn't realize it was killing us.

Then the pandemic arrived.

Covid-19 didn't cause the unprecedented burnout and exhaustion that touched nearly every industry in the early part of this decade: before anyone had ever heard of Covid-19, two out of three workers reported being burned out at work. The pandemic just took an already exhausted, stressed-out workforce and broke it. Like a powerful engine that's been allowed to redline for too long, when we needed to hit the gas and ask for more, the whole thing gave out. It led to workers everywhere doing what had once only been a fantasy. They did what Joyce did, and they did it in numbers never seen before.

They quit.

The Great Resignation

In 2021, Americans quit their jobs in record numbers. More than forty-seven million US workers voluntarily left their positions that year. This number does not include terminations or retirements. Restaurant workers quit. Retail employees quit. Hospitality workers quit. Employees were quitting everywhere but especially in the middle of the country. Workers quit in the largest numbers in Kansas, Idaho, Nebraska, and Texas. Prime-age workers between twenty-five and fifty-four quit. Teenagers quit. Men quit, but even more women quit. Exhausted from two years of crushing Covid waves, nurses and other healthcare workers quit in droves.

This wave of quitting wasn't restricted just to the US. The UK saw an all-time high of one million job vacancies in July 2021. In Germany, more than 40 percent of companies reported that they were lacking skilled workers.

And those who weren't quitting were thinking about quitting.

A slew of polls released in 2021 and into 2022 indicated that at any given moment, 50 to 70 percent of workers were considering quitting their jobs. As months passed, many pulled the trigger, with each month's "quit" numbers—as tracked by the US Department of Labor's Bureau of Labor Statistics—matching or increasing the totals of the previous month. The impact of this employee exodus was felt nearly everywhere. What began as a wave of quitting became a plague* of understaffing. Across the US, business owners posted jobs and "Help Wanted" signs. Food service and retail locations began offering sign-on bonuses and flexible scheduling to attract candidates. Some companies offered cash and gifts just for attending an interview.

It wasn't enough. Workers couldn't be found, cajoled, or bought. By the fall, the number of unfilled job openings in the

---

* I'm sorry about that. I tried five different words here to avoid using a disease-affiliated adjective, but none worked. Forgive me.

US had ballooned by 60 percent. Next to their "Now Hiring, All Positions!" signs, restaurant owners were forced to tape crudely printed notices that said "Short-staffed. Unable to open until 4 p.m." At bars, diners, and retail stores, managers and skeleton crews worked absurd hours to cover staffing deficits. As the country began opening back up and demand for various shops and services returned, customers found longer waits and slower service. A rise in outlandish consumer behavior followed, flooding social media with videos of customers lashing out at workers for all sorts of perceived slights. Next to their "Help Wanted" placards, and taped paper signs adjusting hours, managers posted a third sign imploring customers to "please be kind to those who showed up."

This tide of workers leaving their jobs came to be known in business and media as "the Great Resignation." The term was unintentionally coined by an organizational psychologist and associate professor of management at Texas A&M University named Dr. Anthony Klotz. What's remarkable is that he didn't apply the label to something he *saw* happening. In May of 2021 he did an interview with *Bloomberg Businessweek* and accurately *predicted* what came to unfold months later. "I don't know why I said 'great,'" Klotz told *Business Insider* later that year. He said he had been using the phrase at home in conversations with his wife about what he thought would happen in the workforce. After his interview with *Businessweek*, the label stuck, especially as month-over-month resignations piled up. In breathless coverage that unfolded in print, television, and digital media outlets for more than a year, pundits and experts of every stripe couldn't stop talking about the Great Resignation.

In subsequent interviews and op-eds, Klotz explained what was taking place and how he was able to see it coming. He observed two key factors that would lead to the rise in resignations. First, after increasing steadily since 2009, he noted that the number of quits in the US had decreased in the early months of the pandemic. "When there's uncertainty, people tend to stay put, so there are pent-up resignations that didn't happen," he said. People hadn't changed their minds about quitting, they were just holding off. The other factor is what Klotz called "pandemic epiphanies." "The pandemic... forced many of us to re-evaluate what's important in our lives," he said. Faced with risk, stress, death, and burnout, he predicted that people would question where they were working, what they were doing, and how their jobs fit into their lives. His prediction proved accurate. "The pandemic has made many realize their job does not contribute enough—or at all—to their pursuit for happiness and meaning, and they have decided to invest their energy elsewhere, in new jobs, new careers or in other aspects of their lives."

As foretold, the Great Resignation had arrived—forty years in the making. The one thing Dr. Klotz didn't get right, though, was the label. "The Great Resignation" was an inaccurate term. Quitting, it turns out, was only half the story.

The Great Upgrade

As the pandemic dragged on in 2021 and "the Great Resignation" received widespread media coverage, hiring data brought clarity to what was happening in the workforce. People weren't just quitting their jobs. They were *changing* jobs.

While a small number of people retired and others started freelancing, the majority of those who left a job in 2021 did so to go to a *different* job. In the US, the Department of Labor's Job Openings and Labor Turnover Survey (JOLTS) regularly showed hiring *exceeding* quits in all sectors of the economy.

While lower-paid jobs in restaurants and hospitality had historically high quit rates, they also had historically high hiring rates. In fact, across industries, hiring rates exceeded quit rates in 2021. Across the board, those people who were quitting their jobs were doing so to take better jobs.

That's why, as a label, the Great Resignation is a misnomer. A more accurate title would be to call the trend the Great *Upgrade*—which is exactly what a White House economist called it the following year.

The label isn't the only thing many got wrong. Perception of the timing is out of whack too. The rash of voluntary quits receiving widespread attention in boardrooms and in media isn't new. It's actually been going strong for more than a decade.

According to JOLTS data, the number of voluntary quits in the US more than doubled in the last decade, from 23.1 million in 2011 to 47.4 million in 2021. Resignations didn't unexpectedly spike as a result of the pandemic (though 2021 did bring an all-time high); voluntary quits have risen steadily year over year since the recession of 2008. By 2019, twenty-seven out of every hundred workers quit each year. One study released that year (pre-Covid) predicted that one out of every three workers would quit by 2023. In fact, the US economy was expected to see over forty million quits in 2021, whether there was a pandemic or not.

So, let's be clear: the Great Upgrade, as it should be called, has been around for a decade, has increased year over year, wasn't caused by the coronavirus, and is expected to continue until who knows when. This is not a blip or a fad. Staffing challenges and candidate shortages are here to stay and, in most industries, will get worse.

Why so much switching? Some point to baby boomers leaving the workforce, creating openings for younger workers to upgrade their positions. Others note that in the decade prior to the coronavirus pandemic, the US had a record 110 consecutive months of job gains, adding nearly twenty-two million new jobs to payrolls. Opportunities to upgrade have been plentiful. More than anything, though, the job switching taking place among so many for so long wasn't just about upgrading a job. What workers then and now are chasing is an upgrade to their quality of life. For some, a job change was about an upgrade in pay. For others, they went looking for an upgrade in schedule, or commute, or work location. For some, the pandemic epiphanies Dr. Klotz predicted led them to seek out work that was more fulfilling or had greater meaning. Others could no longer stomach the suffering they had endured for so long and went looking for something better. Though workers switched jobs for different reasons, they were almost all in service to the same want: a job that is a better fit for the life they want to live.

The pandemic gave many workers a glimpse of a life they never thought possible. Among those forced to become remote employees, working from home gave them more freedom and autonomy than they ever had before. With long commutes removed, these employees now had time to cook dinner, exercise, or help their kids with homework. The daily slog of business attire and microwave lunches in the break room was replaced by the comforts of home. When, after nearly two years of remote work, employers mandated that team members return to crowded offices, long commutes, and static schedules, many said "no way." One job-changer I spoke to summed it up this way:

> I'm getting more time with my kids. I have space in my life for exercise and rest. The pace of my life is slower, my stress burden is lighter, and my general demeanor is

happier. My new job is making it possible for me to live a better life, and I'll do whatever it takes to preserve this now that I have it. I'm never going back to the kind of soul-crushing grind I lived with before.

More than anything, though, much of the job upgrading in the last few years has been driven by workers being really, really tired.

Workers are tired of working demanding jobs for wages that barely pay the bills, or don't at all. They're tired of a job whose long hours mean missing important moments in their kids' lives. They're tired of rude customers, bad bosses, crappy schedules, long commutes, tiny cubicles, crummy benefits, and no training. They're tired of being on a team with abrasive leaders, toxic co-workers, low morale, crushing workloads, and no prospects for advancement. They're tired of earning millions for their employer but only getting a raise that doesn't even cover inflation. They're tired of a job that doesn't end when they get home, that leaves no time for exercise or sleep or play. They're tired of spending most of their waking hours prepping for work, going to work, working, leaving work, catching up on work at home, and then going to bed early to survive the next day at work. In short, employees are tired of having to work so very hard all of the time at jobs that are so very hard all of the time. People have looked at their lives and said, "I'm tired of being constantly tired." This is a life lived by many for too long, and people have had enough. As Brené Brown said, "I've never met a single person... that had a joyful, wholehearted life that was miserable at work."

It is this desire for an upgrade to quality of life that is the foremost priority for workers nearly everywhere. And so, we find ourselves at a reckoning. How work fits into our

What workers
are chasing is an
upgrade to
their quality of life.

---

lives is undergoing a massive shift. It started slowly, more than a decade ago, but is now happening at warp speed. Your talent pool is smaller than ever. Employees and candidates are more discerning than ever. They simply will not stand for a less-than-ideal employee experience. At the same time, competitors in your industry are doing what they can to engineer a better employee experience to steal your best workers, while companies in other industries are getting creative by drawing talent from new and different places. In other words, employees are desperately seeking Employalty, and they're beginning to find it.

While this may sound like a deluge of bad news for employers, the truth is it's good news. Because if talented, experienced professionals in your industry are out there looking for an upgrade, it means your company can upgrade too. Never in the modern era of work have there been more talented, experienced employees willing to make a professional switch. If you can offer what is both in demand and hard to find—an employee experience that prioritizes the needs and wants of a changing workforce—you create an astounding competitive advantage when it comes to hiring and retention. An upgrade in talent, then, results in an upgrade in the quality of the products and services your organization delivers and the customer service your clients experience. With higher quality and better service come upgrades to your revenue, market share, brand perception, and profit.

This is the Employalty way. In an era of professional upgrading, the surest path to success is to be the upgrade.* Engineering your employee experience to align with the changing needs and values of the workforce, therefore, isn't just about doing something altruistic. It's a business decision.

---

* I feel like #BeTheUpgrade should be a thing. Go ahead, try it. Tag me: @joemull77.

A strategic one. It requires you to understand that finding and keeping devoted employees in this new age of work is not about fixing people.

It's about fixing work.

This starts with rehumanizing the workplace.

4

Rehumanization and the Myth of Lazy

IN DECEMBER 2021, Vishal Garg, the CEO of the digital mortgage company Better.com, laid off nine hundred employees all at once in a two-minute-and-thirty-three-second Zoom call. Employees had been invited to the unscheduled meeting just minutes before.

"I come to you with not great news," he said. "If you're on this call, you are part of the unlucky group being laid off. Your employment here is terminated, effective immediately." He thanked the employees, said they'd get an email from human resources, then ended the call. The fired workers shared their stunning experience in news interviews and on social media. Some called it a "gut punch" while others described the nightmare of being laid off just weeks before Christmas. In comments to CBC radio, Christian Chapman, a forty-one-year-old underwriter and father of five, said, "It was surreal. My mind was having a hard time processing the words."

Among the many reasons employees didn't see it coming is that business at Better.com was, well, better than ever. In fact, just one day before the mass layoffs, the company received $750 million in cash from a key investor as it announced it was going public. You read that right: *the day before.* Also, many of the fired employees had recently gotten high marks and raises during annual performance reviews. At the time of the call, the company had $1 billion on their balance sheet and an implied total valuation of $6.9 billion. Yes, billion—with a "b."

The two-minute Zoom layoff call wasn't just the tone-deaf choice of a bumbling CEO, however. In the media backlash and news reports that followed, it became clear that the organization operated with a cold disregard for how its business decisions impacted employees. For one thing, the firings were carefully planned. Garg admitted that the company had begun reviewing productivity data and other metrics four weeks before the layoffs. And minutes after the virtual call ended, the laid-off employees found themselves locked out of their computers, phones, email, and messaging. According to Chapman, "It was callous. It was cold. It was premeditated." He went on to say that despite being through layoffs before, "I've never seen a layoff handled that way. I've been in the mortgage industry for twenty years and it blew me away."

Amid a chorus of online criticism following the call, the CEO temporarily stepped away from his duties. Around this time, the CFO of the company released a statement defending the firings, touting the need for the company to have a "fortress balance sheet" and "play offense" in the market. As public outrage intensified, the CEO disparaged those he terminated on an online forum, claiming that the fired workers were "stealing" by working only two hours a day but clocking in for eight or more, providing no proof of the claim. In a final act of you-can't-make-this-stuff-up, some days after these nine hundred employees were fired, many received a holiday package from the company that included a certificate, a trophy, and a company logo T-shirt. After one month away from the role to "reflect on his leadership," Garg returned as CEO.

Better.com's decisions before and after the layoffs demonstrate a painful lack of humanity. Sadly, this is not an isolated incident. In April 2020, cosmetics giant Sephora laid off more than three thousand employees, many over conference call. One month later, WW International, the company formerly known as Weight Watchers, fired a large number of employees over Zoom. And just two weeks after the widespread backlash created by the firings at Better.com, upscale retailer Williams-Sonoma did nearly the exact same thing, firing a hundred seasonal workers in a single video conference call, without notice and before their contracts were up. In response to an outcry from some, Williams-Sonoma remained unapologetic, claiming there is "no fixed time frame" for the termination of seasonal staff.*

What's appalling here isn't that people were laid off. Companies at times need to trim payroll and reduce their staffing levels. Though unpleasant, it is a fact of life in business. It's *how* these people were terminated. These companies skipped one-on-one conversations, certainly as a way to save time, but also because those imposing the layoffs wouldn't have to suffer the discomfort of delivering awful news to so many families. They also gave no advance notice that workers' employment would be ending, so families had no chance to start preparing financially. In these calls that lasted only minutes, they allowed no time for workers to process the announcement or ask questions. They turned a camera on, made the announcement, then turned the camera off,

---

* A spatula on the Williams-Sonoma website costs $38. Their layoffs shouldn't be the only thing sparking an outcry.

disconnecting from the meeting *and* the human cost of what had just happened. These workers were thrown away, discarded at the curb in seconds, like a box of old cassette tapes.

By the way, a note about layoffs to anyone responsible for the employment of others: We should never get comfortable with them. They should never be anything but gut-wrenching. When you initiate layoffs, you create food insecurity. You jeopardize the life-saving medication and treatment covered by someone's healthcare. You inject devastating stress into homes and marriages. You put lives in danger. Layoffs are a fatal violation of the first and most basic promise you made to everyone you ever hired: to provide them employment. There is both a formal and implied agreement when an employee signs on to work at your company. Yes, you're agreeing to an exchange of compensation for productivity, of employment for expertise. But you are also making the promise of security. Employees are trusting you with their livelihoods, their ability to feed their children, to pay for medicine, and to heat their homes. When they say yes to your job, they're saying no to the security of *all other jobs*. They are placing the stability and quality of their very lives in your hands. Layoffs are the price the innocent pay for the poor business decisions of those who, despite their failure, usually get to stay. Our legacies as people, as leaders, and as whole companies are often made by how we care for those closest to us. Layoffs should always be a last resort. For leaders, layoffs should be agony.

In the aftermath of the video conference firings initiated by Better.com, Sephora, WW, and Williams-Sonoma, it's hard not to wonder, *How does this happen?* How do educated, accomplished leaders in visible roles at public companies operate with so little compassion? What caused the leaders of these organizations to act with such callous disregard for people?

Answer: Dehumanization.

The Era of Dehumanization

Dehumanization is the perception and treatment of people in ways that ignore and diminish their intrinsic worth as humans. In the workplace, dehumanization occurs when workers are viewed solely based on their role or functionality. According to Dr. Karen Fiorini, a researcher in humanistic management and organizational change, dehumanization is common and normalized in the workplace. "When a leader values the work and not the whole person, it becomes much easier to increase workloads and expectations because the person's life outside of work is nonexistent."

It's easy to understand why dehumanization shows up in workplaces. Leaders often must make hard decisions that impact peoples' lives. It is understandable that they would engage in psychological distancing and reduce their own empathy as a kind of leadership coping mechanism. But doing so creates a domino effect of suffering, the kind that many workers have endured for years, are renouncing today, and that is entrenched in the culture of organizations that are struggling to find and keep employees.

For one, dehumanization leads us to think of employees not as persons, but as a commodity. We refer to our workforce as "human capital."* We rationalize that it's acceptable to have people on our teams and not remember their names. We hear leaders say that "everyone is replaceable," when literally *no one* is replaceable, because no two people are the same. In organizations where employees say they feel like "just a number" or "cogs in a wheel," dehumanization is likely involved. One of the more brazen public examples of dehumanization at work occurred in March 2022 when an

---

*   I loathe this phrase. Every time I hear it, it's like biting into a rotten apple.

executive at an Applebee's restaurant franchise chain sent an email blast to a group of store managers. In it, he celebrated inflation and rising gas prices for creating economic challenges that would drive more potential employees into the hiring pool. This executive suggested lowering wages, since demand for jobs might increase. He then acknowledged that Applebee's employees often need two jobs to make ends meet. Rather than expressing concern about poverty or the inhumanity of having to work sixty to eighty hours a week just to get by, he advised managers to get their scheduling done early "so [employees] can plan their other jobs around yours."*

When we perceive employees as producers first, people second, we stop feeling compassion toward them; we stop caring when others endure hardship or feel pain. Over time, dehumanization leads to the normalization of suffering, which, in turn, results in the exploitation of that suffering. Businesses routinely choose financial prosperity over the well-being of people as a result. In any case where an employer or supervisor operates without regard for the negative impact a decision, policy, or situation has on an employee, that worker is being victimized by dehumanization. When we don't stop to consider the negative impact someone's job has on their life outside of work, we could end up subjecting them to cruel or degrading experiences. Dehumanization also results in us rarely considering that we, as leaders, are doing anything wrong.

Years of dehumanization have created a gut-wrenching reality across nearly all kinds of businesses: the normalization of inhumane employee treatment. We now live with a multitude of entrenched, normalized workplace experiences—

---

* In response, several store managers quit Applebee's that day. The company disavowed the email and fired the franchise executive.

Workers are
renouncing the
normalized
dehumanization
that's been
entrenched at work
for years.

_____

many brought about by dehumanization—that create suffering, inflict harm, and reduce quality of life for employees. Mass layoffs via short video conferences certainly qualify, but there are many others. Handing out work schedules only days ahead of time, as often happens in restaurants and retail workplaces, is inhumane. After all, how is someone able to plan anything in their life with such limited notice about when to be at work? So, too, is promising a certain number of hours to a worker, then reducing them. This creates a financial shortfall, inflicting economic stress on the household. Similarly, telling employees that they must work for a year before accessing benefits or paid vacation is inhumane: expecting people to work for twelve consecutive months without needing a day off or healthcare is absurd. And expecting employees to stand for seven hours a day in their job is inhumane. It inflicts physical harm. Trust me, no one will stop shopping at your grocery store if the sixty-year-old cashier ringing up their cereal and eggs is sitting on a stool. The same is true for workplaces that limit or discourage bathroom breaks. These are cruelties often reserved for the lowest-wage workers among us. Can you imagine telling an accountant that they are required to stand at their desk all day or that they are only permitted to go the restroom at a specific time?

Speaking of low wages, not paying employees a living wage—one that ensures access to adequate food, clothing, housing, transportation, and medicine—is inhumane. So is expecting employees to be on call during off hours without pay, apprentice for substandard wages, or pay for required training as a condition of maintaining employment. Unmanageable workloads that constantly require extra work after hours or that routinely force employees to miss time or events with family are inhumane. Creating second-class citizens at work is also inhumane. This happens when some employees are given privileges or special treatment not available to all. If some in the company are allowed to get away with things (that others can't) because of what they do, who they know, or the dollars they produce, you're creating second-class citizens. Relatedly, tolerance for any kind of bullying, belittling, hazing, or harassment is, of course, inhumane.

In nearly all of the examples above, people suffer. Yet many workers must comply to remain employed, and so they do. Perhaps the saddest form of dehumanization is that which is self-inflicted. As Dr. Fiorini observed in her research, many workers often don't question whether workload expectations are reasonable or not. They just do whatever it takes to get it done, even at great personal cost to their well-being and even when it affects their family. Workers eventually dismiss the ongoing suffering as normal, saying that it "comes with the territory." Maybe this reaction is born out of the stories employees told themselves for years, about why they endured the very things so many are now pushing back against: For a few, putting in long hours, missing family time, skipping vacations, taking on more and more, and being accessible 24/7 were necessary to demonstrate dedication at work. Over time, some of those who withstood this suffering eventually wore it as a badge of honor, insisting that those who came after should have to "pay their dues" in the same way.

But there's one other consequence of dehumanization that may be the most pervasive and harmful. It's certainly the greatest legacy of a generation of dehumanization in the workplace. It's a phenomenon that reared its ugly head loudly in the months following the arrival of the Covid-19 pandemic but has been persistent for years. It's the belief by a portion of society that those who would no longer subject themselves to dehumanization at work—and the suffering it creates—are actually of flawed character. As workers in greater numbers refuse to stay in jobs that perpetuate the kinds of suffering outlined above, some have come to describe them as being disloyal, not dedicated, or lacking grit. They are called greedy, selfish, or entitled. It's a degrading, misinformed set of beliefs that I've come to call the Myth of Lazy.

The Myth of Lazy

Remember Joyce, from Chapter 3? She was the Practice Administrator who resigned after seventeen years of faithful service, only to have her bosses question her work ethic. After nearly two decades of overwork, Joyce's bosses saw her departure as stemming from a character defect. They blamed her. Their reaction is appalling, but it isn't surprising. Decades of dehumanization of the workforce leads to judgments that are rooted in bias and ignorant of the full humanity of a person.

Joyce isn't the only employee whose character was questioned when she finally took steps to leave an unhealthy work situation. Generations of employees have been subjected to similar treatment. One of the more ubiquitous observations that continues to get bandied about is that "no one wants to work anymore." I'm certain you've encountered this sentiment online, in conversation, or even, for a time, on signs posted by business owners and managers announcing staffing shortages at their places of business.*

As we've already outlined in great detail, over decades many jobs morphed into something bordering on unbearable. As revenue, profits, executive compensation, and shareholder

---

* In fact, the act of posting this baseless statement for customers to see was so widespread a few years ago that it became a popular online meme.

value have skyrocketed, nearly every aspect of the employee experience has gone in the opposite direction. People have been forced to work longer hours with fewer resources, doing more demanding jobs, for reduced benefits, less job security, and stagnant wages. In what amounts to a transactional relationship—the exchange of skills and effort (from an employee) for employment and compensation (from the company)—one side has been getting hosed for years. Yet the moment a worker dares to suggest that this exchange is out of balance and that they are worthy of something more or better, they get labeled by some as greedy, lazy, or uncommitted.

That's delusional.

The only thing that is lazy in this equation is the accusation that "no one wants to work anymore." It's devoid of any insight or critical thinking. It's certainly not backed up by data. At the time of this writing, unemployment in the US is below 4 percent. There have only been three months in the last fifty years when it has been lower. The labor force participation rate for prime-age workers, those twenty-five to fifty-four years old, is higher now than it was ten years ago. Those who hold on to the belief that there is a population-wide character defect causing staffing and retention issues across industries are doing some serious mental gymnastics to put the blame on workers. It's akin to an abusive spouse repeatedly committing an act of violence on their partner, then blaming them for wanting to leave and saying, "you just need to toughen up."

One of the most harmful lies some leaders believe is that workers have gotten soft, that work ethic has declined, and that when some workers push for more it's because they're entitled. These people want so badly to blame workers for a character defect when the defect is the job itself. Or as one business coach, writing in *Forbes* magazine, put it in response to a group of CEOs proclaiming that no one wants to work anymore, "maybe people don't want to work for you."

"No one wants
to work anymore" exists
as one of the most
tired, inaccurate
generational tropes in
human history.

———————————

The Myth of Lazy is almost always hurled at a combination of younger (younger than the accuser, at least), lower-wage, and less educated workers. The simplistic thinking is that if you are at a lesser professional station in life than you want to be, or you are experiencing less than ideal working conditions, then you haven't wanted something different badly enough. The Myth of Lazy assumes that the only thing standing between you and prosperity is *you*, and so its subscribers declare to these folks, you need to "work harder" or "better yourself." This is trite bumper-sticker thinking built on the long-debunked belief that people everywhere have equal access to a ladder of success. It ignores the circular constraints of many limiting factors—like poverty and access to childcare—that can be impossible to escape. And so, the Myth of Lazy not only inaccurately assigns character defects to those who are often doing the most and receiving the least, it also disregards a multitude of social, economic, gender, and racial barriers to upward professional and economic mobility that have existed for generations. Perhaps the most loathsome outcome of the Myth of Lazy is that many workers get blamed for the very suffering they endure. The belief is that if someone isn't visibly working their way *out of* lower wages or arduous labor, they are essentially self-selecting *into* these circumstances. In other words, if someone is in an undesirable situation, it's their own fault for not getting out.

What's most stunning about this mindset, though, is the hypocrisy hiding in plain sight. As workers leave their jobs—seeking better wages, better hours, and better cultures—they are doing exactly what those who subscribe to the Myth of Lazy have long insisted was lacking. They are taking action. These workers are clawing their way to better circumstances, and in response their former bosses are posting signs on doors declaring that "no one wants to work anymore." But this isn't new. "No one wants to work anymore" exists as one of the most tired generational tropes of our existence. Rooted in bias and inaccurate in its declaration, it's been derisively hurled at generations of workers forever. Paul Fairie, an instructor and business researcher at the University of Calgary, recently documented the history of this phrase in archived newspaper clippings. He found examples going back more than 128 years.*

In reality, people are willing to work hard under the right conditions. They just don't want work to be excruciatingly hard all the time. Most people will be quite dedicated at work when their jobs allow them to use their talents, pay their bills, save a little, live a little, spend time with family, take the occasional vacation, and attend to needs at home when they arise. Is that really so much to ask?

Sadly, as jobs go, these kind have become few and far between. When people land in such a role, they immediately recognize it for what it is. It's like winning the lottery. In a sea of job misery, these lucky souls find themselves holding a golden ticket. When employees look around and see that they are treated humanely, paid well, make a difference, use their strengths, have a Great Boss, and enjoy balance between their time at work and away from it, most can't wait to go to work. And when they're there, they respond with effort. They do hard things. Lazy is nowhere to be found.

Rehumanize the Workforce

When leaders get comfortable with any kind of employee suffering, they create workplaces that drive people away. Finding and keeping devoted employees and continually activating their

---

* See also: "These kids today are entitled…" and "This new music isn't even music…"

emotional and psychological commitment at work requires, at a minimum, a more humane employee experience. The rest of this book will focus on creating the conditions that activate emotional and psychological commitment at work, but none of that will matter if what you believe about employees is rooted in cynicism. That's why this chapter had to come now. After all, every employee's quest for a job that allows for a better quality of life is also a search for a workplace that recognizes and honors their complete humanity. For some business owners and leaders, this will require a shift in mindset and beliefs.

The first shift is in no longer treating workers as a commodity. Instead, we must see them as whole and individual persons. As Dr. Fiorini suggested in her dissertation, "Dehumanization in the Workplace," people should be treated "foremost and fundamentally as persons who have individual hopes and dreams, aspirations, worries, fears, personal values, and world views." Along with this should come the belief that work should have as minimal a negative impact on employees' lives outside of work as possible. We should aim to reduce and ultimately eliminate all of the entrenched systems, policies, and belief systems that inflict suffering on employees. That may mean spending more, keeping less, and growing more slowly. It may mean gracefully allowing someone to leave for a better opportunity outside of your organization. These are sacrifices we make as business owners and leaders that, though they often come with a cost, are short-term expenses that are more than made up for in the long run. We should aspire to a place where we're never asking an employee to prioritize their job ahead of their family or well-being. As leaders, our primary job above all others is to keep employees safe. That sacred duty certainly extends to how someone's job interacts with the rest of their life. As doctors adhere to a "do no harm" oath, so, too, should leaders and business owners.

We must also resist blaming employees when our employment experience fails to meet their needs, causing some to move on or preventing others from joining in the first place. For too long, many business owners and leaders have operated as if employees should just be grateful to have a job. If cutbacks, workload increases, pay cuts, abrasive bosses, intractable schedules, rude customers, or stagnant wages have caused people to leave, the problem you're facing isn't about character or work ethic. If you are struggling to fill positions in your company, you don't have a staffing shortage, you have a good jobs shortage. Create positions that are more appealing to workers (more on how to do this in *all* of the pages ahead) and you'll more easily fill those positions.

We must do away, once and for all, with the Myth of Lazy. There is no data to suggest that there is an entire subset of the population whose work ethic has evaporated. When employees insist on better pay, flexible schedules, or clear boundaries between work and home, they are acting in the best interests of those for whom they are responsible. This isn't character defect. It's character.

Finally, we must operate with a singular conviction: that every person, regardless of their professional station, has worth. We can admire those who have climbed the ladder to success for all it took them to get there while also acknowledging that other people's lack of upward mobility is not necessarily because they lack ambition. As a human being, the vet tech making $13 an hour has just as much worth as the veterinarian making $95,000 a year. While each deserves what they have earned professionally, the lack of an education equivalent to the veterinarian's doesn't mean the tech is less deserving of a life free from suffering. Indeed, the veterinarian will have a much easier time finding and keeping devoted vet techs when he creates the kind of employee experience that minimizes suffering, economic or otherwise. Those techs will go from interested to committed if the vet decides that, rather than exclusively maximizing his own prosperity, he will share some of it with those who work alongside him.

There are many entrenched beliefs about work, pay, and employee expectations that do harm to our ability to create environments that spark commitment. To get all the benefits of Employalty, at some point you must make a choice. You either decide that all but the most successful of people are lazy and selfish, or you decide that every person is, regardless of title or education, worthy of respect and endowed with worth—and that nearly all of them have the capacity for greatness if the right psychological buttons are pushed and levers are pulled. There is simply no way we will ever get an employee's best if their job regularly inflicts pain. If you want devotion from employees, you must first devote yourself to them. If you want the highest level of commitment from your workforce, you must first and consistently commit to them, not just as employees but as human beings.

And the way to do that—the way to make your organization a destination workplace—is to ensure every employee experiences the nine dimensions of an Ideal Job, doing Meaningful Work, for a Great Boss. That's what the rest of this book will show you how to do.

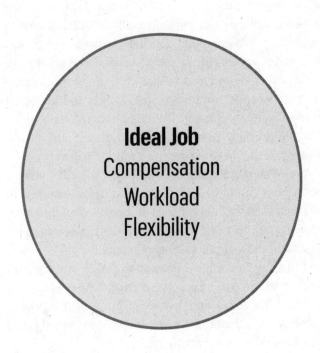

Ideal Job
Compensation
Workload
Flexibility

IDEAL
JOB

5

Compensation

IN HIS TWENTIES, Sean Goode would sleep in his car outside the Home Depot where he worked.

"I would wake up in the morning, put on that orange apron, and show up talking about 'Happy Monday,' 'Happy Tuesday,'" he says. "I know what it's like to have next to nothing." Years later, as the CEO of a Seattle nonprofit, Sean realized he had grown disconnected from that experience. "The further we're removed from a pain point, the less pain we feel. You forget. It happens to all of us." As time passes, promotions unfold, and pay increases, he says, "We forget what it was like when we didn't have it."

Sean is the CEO of Choose 180, a self-described "emergency room for young people in crisis." Choose 180 works to disrupt the school-to-prison pipeline for young Black and brown offenders, particularly boys and men ages twelve to twenty-four. The organization—which employs twenty-four people—was founded in 2011 and began as a partnership between a then-prosecuting attorney and a Black community leader. Through coaching, counseling, legal advocacy, academic support, diversion programs, and other services, the organization has positively impacted the lives of thousands in the greater Seattle and King County area. Choose 180 made headlines in 2022 when it announced that it had raised its minimum salary for all employees to $70,000 a year, a figure that is almost unheard of among small nonprofit organizations.

Despite his own experience with poverty, the CEO admits he did not see the raises as necessary at first. "I said, 'Look, we're already paying above market rate for the roles that we have within our organization.'" At the time, Choose 180's starting pay was $18 an hour. "And that was my justification. But what I was doing was comparing myself to an already inadequate baseline that wasn't providing in the first place," he explains. "It took me a minute to figure out that it was the right thing. It took a lot of pushing by our team and work from our board to help illuminate where some of the inequities are."

Driving the change was an examination of the living wage for those residing in the Seattle area. A living wage is an economic calculation of what a household must earn to avoid a substandard of living. For those who earn less than the living wage in their region, it is expected that they will struggle to access adequate food, housing, childcare, health-care, and more. According to MIT's Living Wage Calculator, the threshold to meet basic needs for a household with one working adult and one child in Seattle is $69,971 a year. An employee starting a full-time job at $18 an hour earns an annual salary of $37,440. "I had to do the same thing my teacher had me do in grade school... a cost-of-living calcu-lation," Sean says. "Figure out what it costs to live in your community—for food, for housing—[and] you can figure out quickly whether you're paying a living wage or not." The CEO realized that many on his team were barely getting by.

"I talked to one of my team members—and she's a single mom who lives in south King County—and I said, 'Do you ever think about buying a house for you and your daughter?' And she laughed at me. She just chuckled, and it broke my heart, because that shouldn't be a laughable moment."

Another team member challenged the organization to consider that their wage structure might be perpetuating the very circumstances they were working daily to overcome. "They said, 'We talk about our young people and how we need to change the material conditions that they're living in because those conditions are what perpetuate the spread of this disease of violence. These inequities... access to quality groceries, childcare, housing instability... is it possible that we're supporting our team members to live in those same material conditions?' That got me over the edge," Sean explained.

To get employees to a minimum $70,000 annual salary would add $400,000 annually to Choose 180's budget. Leadership came to believe they could support the pay increase through a combination of fundraising and grants. With the CEO behind the effort, and the full support of their board, the organization announced the change to its workforce as immediate. "There was a conversation ongoing that people were aware of," Sean says, explaining that some employees knew that a change to wages might be coming. The CEO made the announcement at a regular virtual staff meeting. Some left that meeting with an instant raise of more than $20,000 a year. "It was emotional. In the days that followed, some came and said, 'I can stop driving Uber Eats, I can stop tending bar, I can think about owning a home,'" Sean describes. "A couple of our team members are in first-time home buyer programs now... other folks paid off their cars... It was simply the right thing to do."

Sean and the board at Choose 180 also knew that higher pay would remove other obstacles that can prevent people from being "all in" at work. "Part of the reason [for the pay increase] is that we wanted to professionalize these roles. These people already poured all of their heart into their work. If you work in nonprofit, that's what you do. So we didn't do this in some kind of way to improve performance. This was about honoring their humanity." Sean knew that more generous wages would enable employees to do their work with less financial stress or without having to work other jobs. "In the weeks that followed, our partners were telling us they noticed a difference. Wages aren't a magic bullet to commitment. You still have to develop people, give them tools, coach them... but [with the wage increase] there's a different level of investment. People are energized, but more than anything else, they feel safe."

When I asked Sean what's he's learned since enacting such a notable change, he didn't hesitate to answer. "We could have done this five years ago. It takes somebody to say, 'let's go ahead and do this thing' and step up and step out on faith." Now, Sean and his organization have begun lobbying for a minimum nonprofit salary for government contracts, the way that various trades like construction require. They want to lift all who do nonprofit work, many of whom accept that they are often trading financial prosperity for making a difference in the world. He pushes back on the notion that it has to be that way. "You can't do this work and expect people to be able to provide for themselves if you're not paying them a living wage."

The Wage Gap Is a Canyon

The US is in the earliest days of a wages reckoning that has been decades in the making and has only just begun.

It is being driven by people no longer being able to stay in low-paying jobs in which they cannot earn a living wage.

The concept of a living wage should not be confused with a minimum wage. On the one hand, a minimum wage is the lowest amount a worker can be paid hourly as determined by law. Paying an individual below the minimum wage is illegal. A living wage, on the other hand, is an economic calculation of the lowest possible wage required to sustain a family's livelihood. It calculates geographically specific costs of food, childcare, healthcare, housing, transportation, and other necessities with other factors like taxes and inflation. Because regional costs of living in the US can vary widely—there are significant differences between living in San Francisco versus Athens County, Ohio, for example—it is misleading to calculate a single living wage for the entire US. North Carolina, however, is a lovely stand-in for the broader US. Across thirty-eight demographic, social, and economic indicators— many from the US Census Bureau's American Community Survey—the state of North Carolina most reflects the experience of living and working in the US, in general. So what's the living wage in North Carolina? The lowest hourly rate someone working full-time needs to earn to avoid a substandard of living in the state is $17.14 an hour.

That's for a household of one.

Add a child, and that worker needs to earn at least $33.10 an hour to meet basic needs of food, housing, clothing, transportation, and childcare.* That equates to a salary of $68,848 a year. Yet the minimum wage employers must pay workers in North Carolina reflects the federal minimum wage of the US, which was last raised in 2009.

---

* Want to see more details about how this number is calculated or see the living wage for your region? Visit livingwage.mit.edu.

That minimum wage is $7.25 an hour.

If you run a company in North Carolina and pay a single mother with one child less than $68,848 a year, she will likely struggle to avoid economic distress in one way or another. Given how closely North Carolina reflects much of the rest of the US, the same can be said about many other American locales. While thirty states have minimum wages set above the federal minimum wage, the gap between what companies in the US are required to pay workers and what those workers must earn to live an economically stable existence is still so significant that using the word "gap" drastically undersells the problem. Over the last forty years, that gap has become a canyon.

According to the Economic Policy Institute (EPI), total compensation for the median US worker rose only 10.1 percent since 1979. Yet the cost of living in the US since then has increased nearly 400 percent, according to the Bureau of Labor Statistics' consumer price index. A dollar today only buys 25 percent of what it could buy back then. Adjusted for inflation, the typical male worker earns virtually no more today than his counterpart did forty years ago.

For workers who aren't white males, the canyon is even wider. For one thing, people of color face the lowest pay, the most dangerous conditions, and the fewest advancement opportunities on the job. On average, Black men are paid just $0.71 for every $1.00 paid to white men. Black women, who face both gender and racial barriers, are paid just $0.63 for every $1.00 paid to white men. Indeed, the paltry wage gains of the last four decades have gone mostly to the highest earners, who are mostly white men. Since 2000, usual weekly wages have risen just 3 percent among workers in the lowest tenth of the earnings distribution and 4.3 percent among the lowest quarter. But among people in the top tenth of the distribution, real wages have risen more than 15 percent, to $2,112 a week—nearly five times the usual weekly earnings of the bottom tenth ($426). The highest raises—10 percent or more—typically went to the highest earners, those with annual incomes of $150,000 or more. And higher earners were more likely to have received a raise in the previous year: 67 percent of workers from the highest income group received a raise in the past twelve months, while only 46 percent of people in the lowest income group did. Meanwhile, CEOs are on a whole other planet. The EPI estimates that since 1978, while the typical American worker's compensation has grown not more than 18 percent, CEOs have seen their pay go up 1,322 percent.

The radical disparities between what people earn and what things cost today have created suffering for many in the workforce. One in eight adults and one in six kids in the US experience food insecurity. One in ten Americans have no health insurance. For many, housing costs alone are the bane of their financial existence. In 2020, the average cost of rent in the US was $1,468 a month. For that to cost less than 25 percent of a person's income (a budgeting axiom), they need to make $5,887 a month. For a forty-hour workweek, that's $36.79 an hour. On top of this, childcare costs can be nearly unmanageable. Experts say that to access licensed childcare, a household with two working parents will need to part with 13 percent of their income. For a single parent, it's 36 percent. In most states, putting a baby in a licensed childcare facility costs more than in-state college tuition.*

---

* Affordable childcare is among the biggest economic challenges facing families in our lifetime. It's broken both as a needed service *and* as a business model. See Bloomberg's article "How Child Care Became the Most Broken Business in America."

It is estimated that 58 percent of Americans live paycheck to paycheck and two out of every five American households cannot put any money aside to help them meet an unexpected expense or economic shock. Studies report that as many as 40 percent of Americans are one paycheck away from homelessness. Wages are staggeringly behind and have been for years. Even now, the "fight for 15"—which began in 2012 and saw activists, policymakers, and even legislators advocate to increase minimum wages to $15 an hour—would fall short of lifting people out of poverty. Working full-time making $15 an hour yields an annual salary of just $31,200. If the federal minimum wage in the US had continued to rise with productivity, as it had during the post-war decades, it would be over $20 an hour today.

How did we get here? It's nearly impossible to capture all the economic factors and nuances that answer that question.* Nevertheless, there are several clear influences we can spotlight. One reason for so much income inequality is that US companies in a post-war era made executive salaries and shareholder profits their top priority. Gone are the days of splitting success more evenly between investors and labor. Relatedly, the decline in union access and participation for workers appears to have played a part. Collective bargaining long served as an accountability mechanism that ensured companies shared profits more generously with workers. Others point to the long-term decline in manufacturing employment, which for decades provided relatively high wages to non-college-educated workers, who made up a large portion of the population. And certainly, the increasing costs

---

* Especially since I'm limited to a few paragraphs inside a single five-thousand-word chapter in a larger book about retention and commitment.

of benefits—most notably health insurance—have influenced employers' ability to grow wages.

But more than anything, research from the Economic Policy Institute shows that much of the income inequality workers have suffered these past forty years can largely be credited to policies intentionally designed to suppress the wages of American workers. As the former president of the EPI wrote when discussing their research:

> To be clear, wage suppression was not an unintended consequence—it was the intentional outcome of policies at the legislative, regulatory and corporate levels deliberately implemented to keep wages low. As a nation, we chose to suppress wages on behalf of the rich and corporations—and with spectacular success... The top one-tenth of 1 percent saw their earnings soar at least five times that rate, while median hourly compensation gained only 13 percent and the bottom one-third of workers actually saw their real wages fall. We conservatively estimate that this 43-percentage-point gap between productivity and median compensation— this shift of national income from labor to profits and from the bottom 90 percent of earners to the very top earners—is costing the median American worker nearly $10 an hour—almost $20,700 a year for a full-time worker... As our research reveals, our crisis of radical inequality is not an accident. It is a choice.

Sitting on a pile of cash and given a choice, companies elected to return money to shareholders, grow executive salaries, and limit employee compensation in favor of profits as much as possible. Companies have simply not seen higher wages as an investment that acts in service to their larger goals. And so we find ourselves at a reckoning. After years of limiting pay, where businesses said, *If we pay you more, we won't survive*, the tables have turned. Now workers are telling businesses, *Unless you pay us more, we won't survive.*

Driven in some cases by concern for employee welfare, but mostly as a necessary step to remain staffed and operational, companies have started moving wages more aggressively than in previous decades. Bank of America, the second largest bank in the US, raised its minimum wage to $21 an hour with plans to reach $25 an hour by 2025. Big box retailer Target just enacted a plan to raise its minimum wage to as high as $24 an hour based on location. US wireless carrier Verizon Communications raised the minimum wage of its new and existing customer service, retail, and sales employees to $20 an hour amid a tight labor market and rising inflation. Like Choose 180, KLLM—a large US trucking firm—raised its base pay for over-the-road drivers to $70,000 a year, an increase of up to 33 percent. In media coverage, the CEO said the move was about attracting talent and recognizing their drivers for a job that is challenging.

Where are these organizations getting the funds to boost wages? They're predominantly coming from profits, executive salaries, and new or expanded revenue streams. Amid the Great Resignation, Morgan Stanley, one of the largest investment banks in the world, released a report declaring that "to make up for decades of underpaying workers, companies must roll back their profit margins to where they were 30 years ago."

We should be clear-eyed, though, about what higher wages can and can't do. An examination of much of the literature on the psychology of motivation reveals that compensation has little correlation to sustained higher effort at work. While compensation is a critical component of finding and keeping great employees, it has a minimal impact on the discretionary effort put forth by employees over time.

To move the needle on that factor, you'll need to invest in many of the other dimensions outlined in this book, such as connecting people to purpose and aligning their job roles to their strengths.

There is one exception to this, however—one case where compensation can improve effort: a wages strategy that has become known as generous pay.

Generous Pay

Zeynep Ton is a professor at MIT who studies how to improve operations in industries with low wages and profit margins, like restaurants and retail. In her deeply researched book *The Good Jobs Strategy*, she compared wages between a variety of low-margin businesses and demonstrated, with data, what some business owners might find hard to believe: generous pay to employees often results in more profitable operations.

What constitutes "generous" pay? That's up for debate. If a living wage is the floor for avoiding economic hardship, then generous pay would be a rate that consistently sits above that living wage calculation. To determine the right numbers, some companies are studying employees' net disposable income. In other words, what do employees have left after paying their bills each month? Can they save money? Can they indulge in a vacation from time to time?

This has been the approach of finance technology company PayPal. In 2018, leaders at PayPal discovered that many of their employees had a net disposable income between 4 and 6 percent. They were essentially living paycheck to paycheck with no wiggle room for savings, emergencies, or to enjoy life outside of work. This despite PayPal's wages being at or above market rate for most of their positions. The

CEO set a goal to get employees' net disposable income up to 20 percent, a figure that is often recommended by personal finance experts. To make this possible, PayPal took on a bigger share of employee healthcare costs, raised wages an average of 7 percent, and gave employees stock units. Since instituting the program, the average net disposable income for PayPal employees is near 20 percent, higher than the average American's personal savings rate.

What PayPal's leadership understood is that higher pay is a retention strategy. When companies commit to keeping top talent by paying a bit more, they often end up spending a lot less on turnover, recruitment, and training. In media coverage of their efforts, PayPal CEO Dan Schulman said, "the foundation of moving from a good company to a great company rests upon having the very best employees." The move has paid off. Employee turnover at PayPal has been reduced by half, saving millions in staffing costs. Their customer satisfaction has gone up too. They also report notable improvements in employee sentiment, especially in the number of employees saying they intend to stay with the company.

Such results appear sustainable over time. In 2015, payment processing firm Gravity Payments announced a minimum $70,000 a year salary for its employees. In the years since, the company's revenue has tripled, its customer retention rate sits above 90 percent (far above the industry average of 68 percent), and it has reduced employee turnover at the company by half. Not only that, when they do have openings, they have their pick of the very best talent. Gravity Payments now receives about 25,000 job applications a year for around seventy openings. In the early days of the Covid-19 pandemic, when the company saw a 50 percent drop in business, most Gravity employees volunteered to take temporary pay cuts. The company didn't lay anyone off, and when business returned to pre-pandemic levels, they paid the employees back. These employers are seeing what higher wages and lower economic distress for employees can do. Their turnover is down and commitment is up. In one study, a $1.00 increase in hourly wages resulted in a 40 percent increase in total profits.

Note that compensation involves more than just wages. In addition to higher pay, generous benefits can also have a profound influence on quality of life and, as a result, employee commitment. The most sought-after employee benefits are those that address the very quality-of-life issues that employers are upgrading. Robust vacation time packages, childcare assistance and paid family leave, aggressive retirement contributions, transit subsidies, and concierge services that assist employees with personal errands or unexpected needs are what some employers are using to enhance the total compensation they offer to current and potential employees. According to the Society for Human Resource Management (SHRM), the most sought-after employee benefits are flexibility, health insurance, paid time off, retirement, parental leave, and life insurance.

Businesses of all sizes are using enhanced benefits packages to attract and keep weary workers, especially in those restaurant and retail environments that rely most heavily on lower-wage employees. In addition to raising their base pay, Target is making a $300 million investment in expanded benefits. They're expanding access to healthcare to employees who work at least twenty-five hours a week. They're also adding benefits like physical therapy, acupuncture, and more fertility benefits to their health plan at no cost, and granting access to 401(k) plans earlier in an employee's tenure. At Dick's Drive-In, a West Coast burger chain, the company raised its base wage to $19 an hour while also providing free healthcare, three weeks of paid vacation, 401(k) match, and access to additional annual funds for childcare and tuition assistance. The company's president, Jasmine Donovan, was quoted in news reports as saying that companies that want to be successful must invest profits into employees. "They'll take better care of your customers, which will help you earn more profit. When they move on from your business and do other things, they're evangelists for your company, and that helps you make more profit."

There are several reasons why this happens. First, when you move people out of the circumstance of being underpaid, you remove factors that hinder performance. Zeynep Ton says that when workers spend valuable mental and emotional resources on the worry that comes from financial shortfalls, their cognitive function suffers, which limits their contributions. She cites a double-digit drop in IQ points among people who are constantly thinking about money and making ends meet. However, when employees can operate free from the anxiety of economic distress, she found, they become more capable.

Research also suggests that employers who go beyond a living wage to more generous pay trigger a series of psychological effects that result in higher levels of loyalty and commitment. Wharton professor and organizational psychologist Adam Grant described what happens on his popular *WorkLife* podcast. "I've found in my research that, at work, the majority of people are not takers or givers, but matchers: they believe in giving what they get." Grant says that generous pay triggers a fairness instinct. "People think it's unfair to be underpaid; they're also uncomfortable being overpaid," he says. "If they feel overpaid, they elevate their contributions to restore a sense of fairness." In the long run, employees who experience generous pay are better trained, more engaged, and spend more time helping customers buy products. Companies that commit to generous pay attract a better workforce, which delivers a better customer experience.

Psychology makes it clear that people generally appreciate being treated unusually well. That gratitude influences effort. In other words, generous pay translates to a higher sense of duty and a higher level of effort. What sustains it over time, though, isn't the dollar amount. It's the sense of being valued and taken care of. Pay, in general, is an extrinsic motivator, which research has shown wears off over time. Generous pay, however, appears to spark gratitude, ownership, and loyalty, which drives overall quality and business performance. It also creates scarcity, in a good way, for the company. If I am an employee and perceive that my employer values me in a way that most others won't, or believe that I'm treated better here than I would be elsewhere, why would I consider going anywhere else?

Ton says that business owners and executives must think of employees not as costs, but as assets. "They are the primary driver of sales, profits, and growth." She also found that generous pay works best when it is accompanied by other behaviors that treat employees as whole people worth investing in. This includes caring about their careers, their overall well-being, and the quality of their lives outside of work. These "good jobs," as Ton describes them, appear to require the very rehumanization we explored in Chapter 4 and many of the dimensions that lie ahead of you in this book.* In someplaces, though, it starts with examining whether you're getting compensation right. In the free digital toolkit for

---

* I say again, nearly any research you encounter about what leads people to care and try at work comes back to Ideal Job, Meaningful Work, and Great Boss.

this book, available at employaltybook.com, I have a simple Wages Worksheet you can use to begin an evaluation on whether you are truly competitive in regard to compensation for those in your organization.

Getting Compensation Right

In the new age of work, higher compensation is part of the recipe for attracting and retaining devoted employees. If you want people to join your organization, and stay long-term, you must help your team members overcome the years of income inequality that have left many of them behind. Now, as you'll see throughout this book, for many workers, pay isn't everything. But for some workers, pay *is* the driving force behind job switching, because they have no choice.

For them, it's not about greed—it's about survival.

When a person can't make ends meet, they have to find a way to earn more. Some may ask for a raise or a new role. For others, or in the absence of internal options, it means considering a move to a new organization. After all, the fastest way to an increase in salary is to change employers. If you want employees to be committed, unpoachable, and consumed by the belief that you pay them not only well but better than they would be paid elsewhere, then you must do just that. The math tells us that it's almost always in your best interest to retain an employee instead of hiring and training a new one. Most experts agree that it costs a company, on average, one-half to two times an employee's salary to replace that person.

Getting compensation right in your organization—in a way that plays a part in achieving Employalty and unlocking commitment—will depend on several factors. Budget is

Generous wages
trigger loyalty
and commitment
while saving
companies
time and money
on turnover.

———————————

certainly one. Market forces, revenue, staffing needs, and benefit costs are clearly others. But numbers alone aren't the only aspect of compensation that might need attention where you work. There may also be an obstacle that exists in the ten or so inches between your ears.

There are many beliefs that people have about what some people "deserve" to earn in their jobs. Some of these are tied to education and qualifications. Others relate to experience or the specific value that someone adds to an organization. Often, these beliefs are informed by the markets and industries we operate in.* But what also shapes our thinking about pay are some broken beliefs we hold about ambition and work ethic. There are those that cling to the unflinching and romantic idea that prosperity is available to all if we are simply willing to work hard enough to attain it. But this is magical thinking. For many workers, it's not that the American dream is inaccessible. It's that the race has gotten four times longer. Some are asked to run that race with a weighted backpack, dragging two young children beside them, while others began the race on mile marker ten and had access to a golf cart.

It's the Myth of Lazy at work again. The idea that people who don't earn more just don't want it badly enough ignores more than forty years of legislators and corporations suppressing the wages of low earners while the cost of living has increased by nearly 400 percent. It also ignores the advantages some people had and others didn't. Yes, you worked hard. Yes, you got an education. You took risks and paid your dues. But if you had a middle-class childhood, early access to a computer, food and housing stability, and consistent

---

* I doubt that a restaurant owner would argue that servers should be paid six-figure salaries, for example.

participation in education in a good school district, you enjoyed a considerable head start that not everyone else got.

And yet when lower-wage workers push for higher pay, beyond what their respective professions have typically paid, they are often called greedy or unrealistic. Are we really going to call someone clawing their way to a living wage, trying to provide a better quality of life for themselves and those around them, greedy? As part of your journey to create a more humane workplace, I encourage you to examine your beliefs about what people have a right to earn. Pay attention to where you encounter resistance and question the source of that conflict.

I'm reminded of a physician I met a while back who asked me to settle a debate on what they should pay the Medical Assistants in their practice. In California, where they are based, the average pay was sitting at $20 per hour, and the practice—a specialty provider that required MAs to have a bit more expertise and skill than in other areas of healthcare— was struggling to fill these important roles. I told him that if he wanted to keep his existing talent *and* fill the pipeline with qualified candidates eager to join his organization, that he might want to jump up to a starting wage of $25 an hour to stand out in a crowded market. His face twisted in irritation, and he scoffed immediately, declaring that "there's not an MA alive that's worth $25 an hour!" before he stormed off.

To find and keep the very best talent, employers must shift from a company-first mindset on wages to people-first practices. Gone are the days of operating at the lowest threshold of staffing while paying the lowest wages possible. If you want to unlock all the benefits that Employalty can create, you may simply have to pay people more. Decide that prosperity is no longer the province of owners and executives only. Start by evaluating whether you are paying a living wage. If possible, consider a move to more generous pay. Implement raises that account for inflation; otherwise, you end up paying people less to work than you did the year before. Identify additional benefits and services that enhance quality of life for employees. Get these right, and you're on your way to creating an employee's Ideal Job and becoming a destination workplace. Compensation is the first box to check to seed Employalty.

The next dimension is about the workload employees carry in exchange for that compensation.

6

Workload

DANA KELLY sat behind the wheel of her car in a Burger King parking lot. Her hands were shaking. Her stomach was doing backflips. As tears rolled down her face, she dialed the number in her cell phone.

"By any chance, is that position you offered me still open? Have you filled it yet?"

When the man on the other end confirmed he still had an opening, Dana took a deep breath.

"I want it. If you'll have me, I want to take it."

After the call, Dana collected herself. Then she drove back to her job as a Finance Coordinator and resigned. The day before, she had been given a raise. It didn't matter. Dana had reached a breaking point. Today was the day she would escape from a professional nightmare that lasted seven years, shredded her self-worth, and ultimately landed her in the hospital.

In 2013, Dana took a job as a Payroll Coordinator for an excavation contractor in West Virginia. They had sixty employees and more than $20 million in revenue annually.

And their books were a disaster. "My first year was all about cleaning up a mess and learning how to do it right." She shakes her head, remembering. "At times I was overwhelmed by how really, really hard it was." When she started, nobody in the company knew how to do what Dana had been hired to do. She received no training or orientation. Though she had years of experience as a general business administrator, the position demanded complex accounting knowledge she didn't possess. "More than once I told them I thought they needed to hire someone smarter than me," she laughs.

In every job she's ever had, Dana was known for her work ethic. "I'm always willing to do whatever it takes. I would never want my employer to ever think they weren't getting value out of what they pay me." Accepting her knowledge gap, she threw herself into learning more accounting and righting the financial ship for her new employer. She read books and took classes. She sat with the company's accounting firm, attorneys, and state auditors. She pored over reams of financial documents. At work and after hours, she painstakingly transformed herself into a corporate finance expert. By the end of her first year, she had balanced the company books for the first time in a decade and cleaned up payroll and bookkeeping. She'd also created and documented repeatable systems and quality assurance steps to execute intricate processes and catch mistakes. "I don't love accounting, but I learned it. And I got really good at it."

As Dana's competence and confidence grew, her workload exploded. The owner added companies, handing the responsibility for their finances to Dana. "He'd buy a car wash. He'd start a real estate company. Again and again, it was all handed to me." I asked her how many people would be employed at any other company to do the volume of finance and payroll work that eventually lived with her. "At a minimum, four," she replied. "Most nights, I couldn't get out of there before 7 p.m. I was also in the office most weekends to try and get caught up, but that never happened."

Dana operated like this for years, under constant deadlines, her job bleeding into every waking hour of her life. "I was the only one who could pull finance info, do payroll, pay taxes, or manage the books." Dana saw that being the lone person able to access critical information or execute crucial processes, like payroll, created intense stress and obliterated her work-life balance. "I didn't want it to be that way," she says. "They wanted it that way."

Alongside her vast workload, Dana endured additional suffering almost from day one. She quickly learned that the owner was a rage-aholic. "When he got mad, he would belittle you and scream in a chaotic and insane way. He would punch holes in the wall. Everyone feared him. It was terrifying." As the keeper of the financial knowledge for the company, Dana felt his wrath often. "He didn't understand accounting at all, and when I'd try to explain things, he'd lash out. He'd demean you or call you names or make accusations of theft or dishonesty. I got called late at night once and screamed at because I had put a folder on his desk in a spot different from the one he preferred."

Dana's direct supervisor was also difficult. She took credit for Dana's work but didn't understand her job at all. "She'd constantly question things that were certain—that's the beauty of accounting, numbers are what they are—but it was like gaslighting. She'd relentlessly question what she didn't comprehend to the point of making me question myself." Her boss also insisted that she was too busy to help with anything on Dana's plate. "No one had any idea what she did all day. She shopped online. She took long lunches. Everyone knew. But then she would add steps and processes to my work that made no sense to justify her standing or [make her] feel involved."

On top of an unrelenting workload and difficult leadership, there was a culture of drinking, pranks, and teasing among the team. "There was a lot of juvenile nonsense. Don't get me wrong, I love to have fun and laugh with co-workers, but that's not what this was." Dana told me stories of a never-ending fraternity culture filled with bullying and mean-spirited tricks. Despite being repulsed by the atmosphere, Dana found herself trying to fit in. "It's a strange place to be mentally for an adult, to find yourself trying to be accepted by a group of people who acted in ways you truly didn't like. I felt like a teenager trying to be liked by the cool kids. It led to a lot of anguish."

It also became clear to Dana that others in the company had little knowledge of the volume of work she had each day or the dedication she brought to it. "The accountants would come in and tell the owners, 'you have no idea the amount of work she's done.'" Even so, her supervisor habitually derided her job as "not that hard." Year after year, because she saw all the numbers, Dana watched less-committed employees get bonuses and raises well beyond anything she received. "It's hard to see that the guy who got caught skipping work and going out to breakfast in the mornings got way more than I did. It shatters your confidence to take on more than anyone, and be there more than anyone, and then get the lowest raise. You think, *What's wrong with me?*"

Based on what Dana told us about her experience as an employee, we can complete an Employalty Scorecard that reflects her experience in this position. It looks like this:

Dana Kelly's Employalty Scorecard

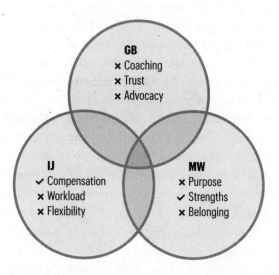

GB
× Coaching
× Trust
× Advocacy

IJ
✓ Compensation
× Workload
× Flexibility

MW
× Purpose
✓ Strengths
× Belonging

Clearly, Dana was experiencing almost none of the conditions that lead to emotional and psychological fulfillment at work. Things came to a head for her in the early months of the Covid-19 pandemic, when she was stunned to find herself laid off. "They told me I could complete most of my duties in one day a week. They said, 'It's really not that much work.'" After just days, ownership insisted that Dana come back. "They said, 'We can't handle this without you,' which was gratifying, yet somehow they remained oblivious to all I had to handle every week." Years of unstable leadership, an insurmountable workload, and the humiliating fraternity culture had taken a toll. "I was physically ill all the time. I also became really resentful. I love people, but I was angry all the time."

Things came to a head that summer when, after a particularly brutal stretch of long hours and deadline-driven work,

Dana had to be taken by ambulance to the hospital with pronounced stomach issues. Years of stress and exhaustion had damaged her digestive system. "I was so sick, but all I could think of was that I had to get out of there to run payroll, which had to happen the next day. Sixty people would be without a paycheck if I wasn't there to initiate it." Against the advice of her doctors, Dana insisted on being released. "I made my husband drive me straight to the office so I could run the payroll. He had to practically carry me up the steps into my office. That's when I had to admit that this job was killing me." Coincidentally, her annual raise took effect the same day. "I remember thinking, *It doesn't matter. The money doesn't matter at all.*"

The next day, Dana found her supervisor once again ambivalent about her workload. "When I told her about being hospitalized, she said, 'Your job's not that hard. If you need to quit, then quit. Everyone's replaceable,' and then she walked out. I just started to cry... Then, I got in my car and drove away. That's how I ended up taking a new job in the Burger King parking lot." For years, Dana had wanted to quit. During her tenure, she had occasionally interviewed for new jobs, even getting offers, only to turn them down. "I don't know why I stayed so long. Yes, the money was good. And I was really good at my job and took a lot of pride in that. In a way, it was like trying to make things work in a dysfunctional family."

Dana gave her boss five weeks' notice. During that month, the leadership at the company repeatedly tried to convince her to stay. "It went from casual comments like, 'you're not really gonna leave...' to guilt, to fear. The owner tried to convince me that the move was career suicide and that my income would be unstable." One week before her last day, she was asked to attend a meeting with the entire leadership team. "They wanted to know exactly what it would take to get me to stay. They said, 'We simply cannot lose you. This cannot happen.' They offered me a huge raise, a private office, an assistant, a new title and duties, and a new schedule. I think if I had asked for an ownership stake in the company, they would have done it." Dana never wavered. She knew that a complete change of scenery was the only path to professional fulfillment and personal healing. Near the end of the meeting, the owner slowly came to a stunning—for him—realization.

"So you're saying there is literally no amount of money we could offer to get you to stay?"

"No," she replied.

He shrugged. "Well then, I don't know what to do with you," he said, and then turned away from her to busy himself with other work on his desk.

In the eighteen months since taking her new role, Dana's previous employer has hired four people to replace her. Their payroll and benefits expenses are more than twice what Dana cost when she worked there. Two of the four positions have already turned over, and the third is imminent. A year and a half after leaving, Dana still gets multiple phone calls every week from her old employer with questions about processes, information, and pressing issues.

To date, the excavation company has tried to rehire her seven times.

So Much Work

I ask audiences constantly: "How many of you have more work right now than you had two years ago?" Nearly every hand gets raised. I then ask, "How many of you would have raised your hand if I'd asked you that same question two years ago?"

Nearly every hand goes up. "And two years before that?" Hands again.

As I detailed in Chapter 3, workers are logging more hours and shouldering heavier workloads than ever before. In both work schedule and work volume, there's been a steady moving of the goalposts for years. In many jobs, the expectation of what one person can reliably accomplish or manage in their role has become unreasonable. Americans now spend up to 19 percent more time on the job than their European counterparts. The average office worker receives 120 emails every day. Even a global pandemic didn't slow the swelling of our at-work obligations. An analysis of the emails and meetings of 3.1 million people in sixteen global cities found that the average workday increased by forty-eight minutes during the pandemic. Lest you think this issue is more pervasive across generational lines, workaholics are now common among nineteen-to-thirty-five-year-old workers, perhaps more so than among older members of Generation X and the baby boomers.*

What's remarkable about the expansion of work is that we've had clear evidence for a while that long hours and stress reduce both productivity and quality. Among industrial workers, overtime raises the rate of mistakes and safety mishaps. For knowledge workers, tiredness and limited sleep impair thinking. As we've spent decades giving employees more work, we've slowly made them less effective. We're also obliterating their health. One research team that looked at long work hours across 194 countries found a higher risk of heart disease and stroke, leading to about 745,000 attributable deaths.

---

* The idea that millennials are lazy is bunk. They've mastered the art of doing what they love and making money at it, something the rest of us didn't necessarily prioritize. That takes extraordinary effort.

Their study called long work hours the largest of any occupational risk factor calculated to date. According to the Centers for Disease Control and Prevention, overwork is linked to weight gain, alcohol and tobacco use, and higher rates of injury, illness, and death.

Dana Kelly's employment experience is extreme—but common. While many factors contributed to her resignation, the biggest and most corrosive factor was her workload and how it subjugated everything else in her life to her job. This is what's at the heart of much of the job switching and upgrading that's been taking place for more than a decade. Exhausted workers have hit their breaking point. They're refusing to sacrifice health and happiness outside of work for success on the job. Parents are resolving to no longer be the last parent picking up their child from school. Managers are swearing off having to constantly do catch-up work on evenings and weekends. The Great Upgrade is about many things, but mostly it's about people wanting their lives to come first. Your organization will have an easier time keeping workers both employed *and* engaged if you can offer them a job that requires them to work less and do less work—in other words, both fewer hours and demands.

Yes, I'm suggesting that you exchange the same (or even more) wages for less work than you have historically.* Don't think of it as a reduction. Think of it as a recalibration, the result of which produces loyal, dedicated employees. In this regard, you'll still come out ahead in the long run. To get there, you'll need to examine both work *schedule* and work *volume*.

---

* Breathe. That's it. Nice and slow. It's not as crazy as it sounds, and it's a path to the workforce of your dreams.

People need
time to think, be
creative, attend
to quality, participate
in learning, and
develop relationships
with collaborators.

———————

Work Less

The decade ahead will likely be known for innovations we haven't even imagined yet. In the workplace, it may be known for the rise of a new way of scheduling employees: the four-day workweek.

As overwork has become a chronic issue, entire countries have started piloting and testing shorter workweeks. Between 2015 and 2019, Iceland ran a series of trials, across industries, to study the impact of switching to a four-day workweek. The trials involved more than 2,500 workers—more than 1 percent of the country's workforce—who moved from working forty hours a week to a thirty-five- or thirty-six-hour week, without a reduction in pay. The pilot participants worked in a diverse array of workplaces including offices, preschools, and hospitals.

The results have been called "transformative" and "groundbreaking evidence for the efficacy of working time reduction."

Across the trials, productivity remained the same or improved in the majority of workplaces. Employees reported lower levels of stress and burnout, and increases in their overall health and work-life balance. The positive shifts in health and mindset weren't just work affiliated. Workers also reported less stress at home and wider social well-being. They described having more time to spend with their families, do hobbies, run errands, exercise, and tend to household chores. In the years following this landmark pilot, trade unions and employers in Iceland worked together to renegotiate working patterns at companies and public service organizations. Now, 86 percent of Iceland's workforce have either moved to a shorter workweek for the same pay or will gain the right to do so.

Since Iceland's project, many more countries have started exploring reductions in labor time across their workforce.

The Spanish government agreed to a thirty-two-hour work-week over three years for its employees without cutting workers' pay. The prime minister of Finland is on record in favor of shortening the amount of time people work, suggesting companies adopt a flexible six-hour day and a four-day workweek. Scotland, Japan, and Belgium have all announced plans to explore a reduced workweek. In Germany—which already has one of the shortest workweeks in Europe at an average of 34.5 hours a week—trade unions are calling for further reductions to enhance retention of personnel. And in Denmark, which consistently ranks among the top three happiest countries on earth according to the World Happiness Report, people rarely put in more than thirty-seven hours a week, often leaving the office by 4 or 5 p.m.

Employers large and small have been experimenting with condensed work schedules for years, but post-pandemic, such initiatives are enjoying more testing and implementation than ever. InDebted, a debt collection agency, moved to a thirty-two-hour, four-day workweek. They started with a pilot program in select teams. After it launched, they received more applicants for open positions in forty-five days than in the previous four months. Overall, the company's average number of applicants has increased 283 percent. Inside their workforce, 98 percent of employees indicated that the new four-day workweek positively impacts their well-being. The four-day workweek has also been embraced by Bolt, an ecommerce developer. Since its implementation, 84 percent of employees said they have been more productive, 86 percent have been more efficient with their time, and 84 percent report an improvement in their work-life balance. Now, the CEO says he "couldn't imagine running a company any other way."

The rise of the four-day workweek has not been limited to tech companies or employers with scores of remote workers. As noted in Chapter 1, Oklahoma LED offers their crews a four-day workweek. Hospitals and other healthcare entities have been offering four-day options to nurses and other staff for years. According to *Newsweek*, Shake Shack, Panasonic, Unilever, and the cities of Boulder, Colorado, and Morgantown, West Virginia, are all currently testing or offering a four-day workweek for employees. Shorter workweeks are popping up in all kinds of industries. "Companies we have helped to make the transition to a four-day week have reported it has significantly expanded their pool of potential recruitment candidates," said Joe O'Connor, Global Pilot Program Manager at 4 Day Week Global, which is running tests of four-day workweeks around the world.

Happiness expert Dan Buettner has reviewed research on more than twenty million people worldwide and has led extensive research in the world's happiest countries. He says, "When it comes to your work, try to work part-time, thirty to thirty-five hours a week." He also finds that six weeks of vacation per year is the optimal amount for happiness. If that isn't possible, he says, employees should at least get to use all of their allotted vacation time and negotiate for more. If the idea of offering your employees thirty-hour workweeks and six weeks of vacation seems out of reach, then operate on the general rule that less is more. A more reachable goal could be just to get slightly below forty hours per week. Research shows that even shaving an hour or two off the standard forty-hour workweek can have huge benefits, both at work and at home. Less than 10 percent of workers are able to achieve that schedule.

But a manageable workload is not just about sticking to a forty-hour workweek or, if possible, implementing a shorter one. It also requires us to manage the workload that employees carry during their allotted work time.

Less Work

When I ask audiences at conferences and events if they have more work now than they did two years ago, I often follow up with two additional questions. The first is, "How many of you have a colleague who decided not to come to this event because they had too much on their plate?" Half of the hands in the room usually go up. Then I ask, "How many of *you* considered skipping this for the same reason or because of what it will take to unbury yourself later after being away for a day or two?" Again, nearly half in attendance lift their hands as many let out a resigned sigh.

One of the clear drivers of job switching in this decade is employees rejecting unrelenting workloads. Dramatic increases in hours, meetings, and duties have left many workers operating in a persistent frenzy. It is a sad commentary on the state of work when professionals in my audiences at conferences acknowledge again and again that it's nearly impossible to step away, even for a single day, to participate in professional development. When the very activities designed to help them learn, grow, and improve are inaccessible because of an unyielding amount of work, something is broken.

In many places, even minutes matter. My company offers a subscription to short, on-demand virtual micro-courses on effectively leading teams. We have organizations from all over that subscribe and whose managers receive the learning content each month. These engaging* videos typically average between eight and twelve minutes in length. When we survey those managers who have never opened or watched the program, the number one reason given is either "I'm too busy" or "I don't have time." I say again that these videos are often less than ten minutes long.

---

*   If I do say so myself.

Part of the problem is that how we define "work" has shifted. As organizations prioritized efficiency and product- ivity, the time workers need—and generally used to get— to create, innovate, build relationships, or participate in development has evaporated. Where a standard workday or workweek would often have peaks and valleys, busy times and down times, many workers no longer experience such ebb and flow. As one manager at a workshop told me recently, "I put fires out every day, and there are always fires. I'm yanked from one crisis to another. Evenings are when I have to do my actual work."

The National Aeronautics and Space Administration (NASA) in the US has studied workload management extensively in recent decades. After all, burnout isn't something mission control wants to contend with when astronauts are manag- ing complex equipment while rocketing through space. Their research has shown that those who are overburdened with work tend to hurry their performance; commit more errors; yield poor accuracy; become frustrated, uncomfortable, and fatigued; and have poor awareness of their surroundings.

However, employees with *not enough work* can be sub- ject to the same outcomes. Low workload has been linked to more mistakes, frustration, fatigue, and poor awareness of surroundings. In other words, when people at work are bored and their attention drifts, complacency sets in. There is, essentially, a sweet spot between *too hard* and *too easy* that we, as employers, should be aiming for. This target area gives employees regular amounts of challenge that align with their knowledge and gifts. It doesn't force them to operate con- stantly beyond the scope of their capabilities, though it might occasionally, and it's mixed with periods of recovery, connec- tion, reflection, and development.

How do you find this balance for your team members? Start by conducting audits of tasks, meetings, and schedules.

Using instruments such as the NASA Task Load Index (TLX) and the Subjective Workload Assessment Technique (SWAT), ask end users to report their perceived workload, then assess the intellectual and emotional toll of different kinds of work. Via interviews, focus groups, or even surveys, identify the work that is most physically or mentally demanding and determine what percentage of people's time they spend attending to that kind of work. A word of caution, though: don't frame these interviews around whether or not the employee can "handle" certain things. Many are bound to say yes, out of fear or pride, but that doesn't tell you whether overwork or burnout are present. Instead, start understanding when their jobs are hardest and when (or if) they get time at work to recover, connect, and learn.

Remember, people aren't robots. We are not built to always run on our max setting until our batteries are completely drained. We have varying degrees of focus. We have emotional peaks and valleys. We need breaks from the most mentally and physically demanding types of work—otherwise we're on a collision course with burnout. In nearly every kind of job, people need time to think, be creative, attend to quality, and do follow-up. They need time to ask questions, attend training, or develop relationships with collaborators. Managers need time to meet with employees, plan and execute staff development activities, participate in conferences, and more. In high-touch jobs that require workers to spend emotional capital—think healthcare workers, counselors, customer service representatives, etc.—cycles of downtime and recovery while on the job are critically important. In jobs where employees experience even short breaks between bouts of their most demanding work, there is improved productivity, less decision fatigue, increased creativity, and employees feel more valued.

Are your employees getting these kinds of breaks? If not, why not, and how can you create more of them in a day, week, or month? By the way, the digital toolkit for this book includes a Workload Inventory Questionnaire you can use to begin these conversations. You can download this tool at employaltybook.com.

Finally, don't underestimate how technology can help you reduce the burden on an employee's ongoing workload. In many organizations, processes and systems are woefully out of date. In places where newer software is installed, the full functionality is often underutilized. While I was leading a workshop for a multisite dental practice, one employee reported that she spends six to ten hours a week on manual data entry and that "it's the bane of my existence." The man sitting *right next to her* was their Director of IT. He was aghast. "Why aren't you scanning the documents and just letting the new accounting software we got last year import all of that?" She looked stunned. "I... I didn't know that was an option... You mean, it can *do* that?" The IT Director smiled. "Yes. I'll sit with you on Monday and show you how. We can get your ten hours a week down to less than one." She looked over-joyed. Then she whacked the IT Director on the shoulder. "Why didn't anyone tell me this *last* year!"

Too little work, and people lack challenge (which is an important ingredient in commitment that we'll discuss more in the Meaningful Work section of this book). Too much work, which has been the case for so many for so long, and people become threadbare. A manageable workload is about striking a balance. Think Goldilocks: not too much, and not too little, but just right.

Once your organization gets compensation and work-load right, you're just one dimension away from creating an employee's Ideal Job. It's time to talk about what is now the most sought-after employee benefit in the world: flexibility.

Flexibility

"**I**'VE GOT an offer for you."

Jack Merrill, Director of Support Services for Trover Health System in Madisonville, Kentucky, stood before his eight-man HVAC team in the hospital conference room. These men didn't know why they had been called to this meeting, but they weren't nervous. Some leaned back in their chairs. Others propped their feet—all in heavy-treaded work boots—onto the conference room table. As a group, they sat with their arms crossed and their hats pulled low, their worn and stained coveralls in stark contrast to the sterile white walls of the meeting space. When Jack spoke, their friendly chatter quickly stopped.

"I know we've lost a lot of guys to the factories in town. I know you can go work for GE and get paid more. I can't compete with that. I wish I could pay you more, but I can't. There is, however, something I can give you here that you can't get there. I can give you more time."

The men in the room stared at their boss, waiting to understand.

"How would you like total freedom to decide when you work, how long you work, and when you don't work? How would you like to be able to schedule around other things outside of work like family time, whenever you want? How would you like to be able to pick up side work for extra money with local contractors anytime you can?"

He had their full attention now.

"The way I see it," he said, pointing to the list he'd made on the whiteboard behind him, "I have to have 100 percent of this work done by the last day of every month."

His list was detailed. This team was responsible for the monthly maintenance of 660 heating, cooling, or refrigeration units in thirty-six buildings across twelve counties in Western Kentucky. The Trover Health System included a hospital, dozens of outpatient clinics, and numerous office buildings. Every month, these men worked in operating rooms, cafeterias, and on building roofs. They maintained MRI and CT scanners. In any place where there was heating or cooling equipment, state regulations mandated servicing and documentation monthly, without fail. In addition to ongoing maintenance, this team was also responsible for all service calls related to heating, cooling, and refrigeration. Whenever something went on the fritz, members of Jack's team got a work order, traveled to the site, ordered parts when needed, and made repairs. Most months, they could barely keep up. They were chronically short-staffed and relied heavily on overtime to stay on top of the work.

"Here's what I propose," Jack told the room. "If you complete 100 percent of the preventative maintenance every month, complete all work orders, and make sure we always have at least one person on for coverage, all without me having to manage any of it, I don't need to know when you're here or when you're not. Schedule-wise, you can do anything you want. You can come and go as you please."

Jack let that last sentence hang in the air. There were no more boots on the table. Now, every man in the room was leaning forward. After a moment of stunned silence, a long-tenured technician asked the question everyone else was thinking.

"What's the catch?"

"No catch, really," Jack replied. "You each gotta average forty hours a week across the month, you gotta get all of this done with no overtime, and you have to manage the whole thing yourselves. No more service calls coming to me. You keep me out of it."

The men in the room looked at each other. Smiles crept across their faces. One by one, they started to nod.

"Oh, and one other thing," Jack offered. "We have to have 100 percent completion, every month. Not 99 percent. Not 99.9 percent. The first time we fail to clear 100 percent of all maintenance and work order requests in a month, this all ends. No excuses. You do whatever it takes."

He didn't know it at the time, but with one conversation, Jack had seeded all the ingredients for Employalty. In the months to come, Jack would witness a complete transformation that supercharged employee engagement, elevated customer service, saved tens of thousands of dollars for the health system, drew the best talent in the community to open positions, and profoundly altered the way he would lead teams for the rest of his career. Most notably, in the ten years that followed that meeting, the HVAC team at Trover Health System never once failed to reach full completion of all their work in a single month.

Employalty through Flexibility

Jack smiles at the memory of that meeting many years ago. "I needed to do something. I was having difficulty holding staff.

Our workloads just kept increasing as regulatory agencies kept adding more codes and requirements. Plus, two local factories were paying 20 to 30 percent higher wages that I couldn't even consider giving. I lost a lot of good people."

Jack's journey to a new model of employment began with a crisis. In one of his departments, he had become so short-staffed that he had to contract with an agency for services. "That's really expensive, but I didn't have a choice. The work had to get done," he says. It turns out, using a contractor was a blessing in disguise. "That's what led to my 'aha' moment." When Jack brought on a third-party contractor to cover some facilities services at the health system, he had no control over when the contractors worked or how they staffed their services. "I wasn't paying them for hours. I was paying them for outcomes. I had a list of things that had to get done each month, and I paid them to complete that list. How they got it done was up to them." For that department at that time, Jack no longer had to manage schedules, stay on top of employees, or even take work orders. The contractor handled it all. This was a revelation, Jack tells me. "I thought, *Why can't I give my staff the same treatment?*"

"We were losing a lot of folks to local factory work, but in those jobs there was a lot of mandatory overtime and weekend work. Those workers made more money, but they had lost control of their lives. They had no time. I thought, *You're not paying your employees for their time. You're paying for a result. If they can get that result in less time, then I can give them that time back and that costs me nothing.* That's how I could compete." As Director of Support Services, Jack was responsible for eight departments, including construction, grounds, property management, environmental services, and biomedical engineering. Collectively he led teams of more than two hundred employees. "I admit, I had trust issues," he says, shaking his head. "I always felt I had to backcheck people's work all the time. I always had the feeling that the staff are just doing the least amount possible to get through the day. I thought it was my job to constantly push people to get work done." His experience working with contractors showed him it was possible to be more hands-off as a leader.

He decided to pilot this approach with one of his departments. "I put a fair amount of thought into this because I really didn't want to unleash something that I'd have difficulty reeling back in. I knew that if I had to shut it down, it would reduce morale even further." Once he got clear on how to go about it, not everyone on his management team thought it was a good idea. "I had some supervisors who were reluctant. They said we were putting too much trust in the employees, that they would take advantage of it, they would cheat the system. I said, 'It's a sweet deal. If they cheat it, we'll just stop.'"

The first thing Jack noticed after launching his pilot with the HVAC team was that he no longer had to spend time managing schedules, distributing work orders, and being "in the weeds," as he puts it. His team took his rule to manage everything themselves to heart. "They managed all monthly maintenance themselves. They had departments call them directly when there was an issue, or a repair was needed. Eventually, if I even tried to ask a question, they'd throw up their hands and say, 'we got this.' They didn't want me involved!" He laughs at the recollection.

In just a few weeks, Jack saw his role shift from managing details to acting as a coach. "I let them make mistakes. I let them fix their problems, rather than swooping in and doing it for them." With fewer details to manage, how Jack spent his time as a leader changed drastically. "By giving them trust and ownership, it allowed me to expand my role into other things that were bigger and better for the organization. I didn't have to spend time chasing people or pushing to get work done. That all went away."

As weeks turned to months, Jack saw a whole host of other benefits and improvements because of his pilot program. "These guys ended up communicating better with their customers, so quality and customer service went up. Teamwork improved too. They had to collaborate and be adaptable together, and it built camaraderie." The morale, energy, and attitude of the whole team had changed as well. "They were so excited because now they could arrange to be at their kids' birthday parties or do side work to make a few bucks when they needed it, or go hunting when they wanted. They could play in the mornings and work at night, or vice versa. But also, they had ownership and influence where before they'd had none. It's hard to explain, but when people stop just doing the minimum to get by, the workload actually shrinks. We were getting everything done, I never had to pay overtime, we were regulatory compliant every single month, and everyone was less stressed and more engaged."

Another outcome of Jack's pilot program was that team members were doing more of what they were good at or found most interesting at work. "They leaned in to each other's strengths because it created more success for the team. They quickly figured out that one guy was better over here and faster at that kind of work, so they had him do more of it. Or someone in a different area would say, 'Hey, I have this strength, can I try this other role?' and they'd let him. And if it worked out, great. When it didn't, he could still go back to his prior work. The staff created a safety net for people to try things and grow."

Even though every employee operates with their own individual scorecard, for expediency, let's think of what the collective Employalty Scorecard for Jack's HVAC team might have looked like prior to his pilot program. Based on what he shared about pay, workload, and his style, it was probably something like this:

HVAC Team's Employalty Scorecard before Pilot

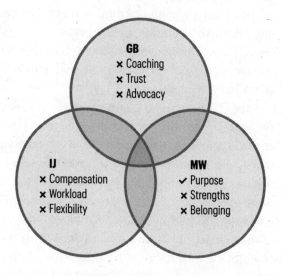

Now consider what the team's scorecard looked like just a few weeks after Jack launched the pilot program:

HVAC Team's Employalty Scorecard after Pilot

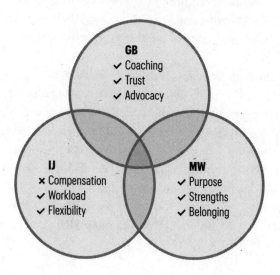

As Jack's approach proved to be a success, he expanded it to his other departments. "After one year, I added our mechanical department. After three years, we were doing it everywhere. Almost every time we started, there would be someone who would say, 'Well that won't work *here*.' I'd say, 'We'll see'—and it did."

Over time, Jack observed another significant benefit to granting his team more trust and flexibility: they became accountable for the quality of the people on the team and the performance each person put in. "Whenever we had a low performer, someone not holding up their end of the deal or making more work for others, the team handled it. They'd put pressure on this person to fix it. We weren't quick to fire people. They knew they had to try and work with them so they'd train them, take them under their wing, do as much as they could. If that person didn't improve after being given every opportunity, the team would come to me and say, 'We can't work with this individual,' and we'd move on." On Jack's teams, a low performer could jeopardize the biggest incentives workers had: time and freedom. As a result, these teams self-policed their culture of high performance. They weren't going to let anyone endanger the autonomy they enjoyed on the job and the quality of life they were experiencing outside of work.

In time, these teams went even further, taking responsibility for bringing quality people into the organization. "I'd have my people coming and saying, 'Hey, I know this guy or this lady, and they're awesome.' These guys started talking outside of work and bringing new people into the organization that were high performers because they didn't want people coming in who wouldn't keep on top of the work. Eventually, I never had to look for new people. I barely had to interview. These guys went out and pulled good people in that they knew would be successful. We became the talk of the town. We became a destination.* I wasn't paying more. I was giving them something more important: quality of life."

When all three factors in the Employalty model are in place in an organization, and when they are each experienced in full by the individuals that make up a team, the company experiences the full benefits. Jack's team had retention (top talent stayed), reputation (talented people wanted to work there), and revenue (savings on overtime and turnover were significant).

Commitment on Jack's teams skyrocketed, he enjoyed a steady stream of quality candidates applying for openings, and he never got pulled into a wage war with the local factories. By granting people more autonomy, flexibility, and freedom, Jack created a transformation. "This has changed my whole approach to managing people. I probably managed the hard way for fifteen years. I made a lot of mistakes. I tried to micromanage and control everything. I didn't want people to think, just do. Once I started treating people like adults and trusting them, everything changed." Jack learned what researchers in the psychology of motivation have known for years. Motivation isn't something you do to people. It's something they experience when the conditions are right.

Flexibility Is about Autonomy

To reap all the rewards made possible by Employalty, remember what I wrote earlier in this book: you can no longer focus on hiring the best person for the job. To attract talent and

---

* Jack used this word during our interview without any prompting. I could have hugged him. #DestinationWorkplace

inspire commitment, you must create the best *job* for the *person*. One of the most powerful ways to do this in your organization is to prioritize flexibility for employees.

Flexibility is now the most sought-after work benefit, according to the Society for Human Resource Management (SHRM). For many workers, flexibility has shifted from being a perk to being an essential job component. In a survey conducted by the Harris Poll, eight out of ten workers said a flexible schedule was important when considering taking a new job. In fact, a flexible schedule is now more important to job seekers than employer retirement contributions and unlimited PTO.* There was a time when offering flexible schedules or work arrangements would give your organization a recruiting advantage. In some industries this is still true, but broadly it is no longer the case. As work flexibility has grown in both popularity and frequency, it's no longer a differentiator. Now, the *lack* of flexibility may result in candidates perceiving a potential employer as out of touch or unsupportive of work-life balance. Why? Because flexibility, in practice, is considerably widespread, with up to 80 percent of companies now offering flexible work arrangements of some kind.

The ability to work from home at least some of the time, often on a schedule they determine, is the biggest form of flexibility sought by workers. In a survey of nearly a quarter of a million workers in 190 countries, 89 percent of people expect to be able to work from home on occasion. This expectation is highest—more than 90 percent—in digital and knowledge-based fields, but it's grown increasingly common in nearly every industry. Even in job roles like manual labor and manufacturing, an overwhelming majority of people said they expect to be able to do some of their work offsite

---

* Though these benefits are still among the most desired by workers.

Flexibility is
no longer a
differentiator.
It's an
expectation.

———————————

in the future. For roles that don't lend themselves to regular work-from-home arrangements—think bedside nurses, flight attendants, or plumbers—flexibility may mean having options related to start and end times, varied shift lengths, work location choices, compressed workweeks, and more. Recognize that at the center of flexibility is autonomy. Giving workers more freedom to influence their schedules, allocate their hours, and determine their preferred work location is becoming increasingly common and will likely continue.

This is an important distinction. Some reduce the idea of flexibility to simply mean hybrid work arrangements. This is a false equivalency. With hybrid, employees typically spend some days on-site and others away, but these schedules are often dictated by the company. In many hybrid work models, employees still lack autonomy. With true flexibility, employees get adaptability. What many crave more than just a hybrid or work-from-home schedule is the freedom to figure out for themselves how, when, and where to work. It is this ability to respond in real time to both unexpected life developments and personal schedule preferences that truly determines whether an employee experiences flexibility.

Take, for example, an employee whose partner is actively deployed in military service. Flexibility might mean allowing that person to throttle his or her work schedule up or down on the calendar depending on their partner's leave schedule. Or consider the father who gets a call from school indicating his daughter is sick and needs to be picked up. In the past, that parent would be forced to leave work and use PTO or forfeit pay to retrieve and care for his child. With flexibility, he can adjust his hours in real time, shifting some work into a different part of the day or week.

Flexibility, in some places, may also mean allowing workers to tune in to when they are most productive. I met the CEO of a software company recently who had just given up the expectation that programmers work a set, daylight schedule. He told his team, "Get done what you need to get done. Do it well and do it on time. *When* you do it is up to you." He told me, "Many of these guys are night owls, so this change had an immediate impact. Their work product got better, it came in faster, and it's made them happier. Autonomous schedule-making is one of the best decisions we've made."

What this software CEO experienced is the same thing Jack Merrill experienced when granting more flexibility to his HVAC team: the quality of their work increased. That's because the more control we each have over our environment, the more intrinsic motivation we experience in that environment. Flexibility—specifically the autonomy employees experience when they get to determine aspects of their work situations—isn't just an essential ingredient to attracting candidates to jobs at your company. Psychology tells us that autonomy is part of how we motivate employees to become committed and do quality work. When members of Jack's HVAC team were granted more control, choice, and influence over their schedules, they took more ownership of their work, which they performed with greater care and attention. That increase in quality was then sustained over time, no paid bonuses necessary. Where workplaces grant employees more flexibility, they can expect a greater degree of satisfaction, fulfillment, and engagement at work.

Engineering Flexibility

The good news is that technology now allows for work flexibility never dreamed of just a few years ago. The coronavirus pandemic forced organizations of all sizes to adopt new tools—like virtual meeting software and digital project management tools—more quickly than they otherwise might

Flexibility can mean options related to start and end times, shift lengths, work locations, compressed workweeks, and more.

_____

have on their own. Microsoft CEO Satya Nadella said the pandemic led to "two years of digital transformation in two months." The result is that many companies now have a high degree of comfort with remote work situations for employees and proof that they can be implemented successfully. The bad news is that flexibility can make some things that were once easy harder, like pulling a team into a quick meeting for an update or problem-solving discussion. However, in most cases these challenges can be solved with more planning and better communication, which are necessary tactics for making flexibility work in any organization. Managing remote teams specifically comes with a unique set of challenges, especially as it relates to camaraderie and building relationships. We'll explore this topic in greater detail in Chapter 10 (Belonging).*

To begin offering more flexibility to your employees, you'll first want to invite employees into that conversation, so you can engineer ideal arrangements together. Communicate clearly about what you are trying to achieve along with what you can and can't do. Tell people, "We know this is important to you and we want to create as much opportunity for it as possible. We also have to keep the front desk fully staffed. How do we create flexibility without compromising operations?" Invite your team to discuss, generate ideas, and test various approaches. This demonstrates your commitment to innovating in ways that enhances their quality of life.

Also, by including your team in evaluating successes and failures, you'll create buy-in for any boundaries or limitations that must exist in regard to your flexible work policies,

---

* To get started, check out episode #63 of my *Boss Better Now* podcast, where we discuss strategies for connecting remote teams in greater detail.

because they too will have seen why they are necessary. Any number of ideas could come out of these discussions. Perhaps you'll create adjusted schedules or staffing patterns for some roles. Maybe you'll end up creating a greater variety of position classifications. Many organizations have gone from expecting everyone to be a full-time, forty-hour-a-week employee to being a company that offers a half dozen different kinds of employment options.

If you want to grant employees more autonomy via flexibility, you and the employee will need clarity on individual expectations and outcomes. This is an ends-versus-means conversation. Define the ends for people in their positions. What should the final output be, and how will you measure that? Also, review any specifics that must exist about how the employee is to execute their work. Then get out of their way and let them determine the means. You'll also need to create systems that keep lines of communication open for teams, while allowing for varied work schedules. Setting an expectation that employees participate in preset touch-base sessions or check communication channels like Slack or email with a certain amount of frequency can be helpful.* Chart out timelines and schedules for projects in advance. Include key meetings and deadlines. Build in update sessions. It can also be helpful to convert larger teams into smaller workgroups. Instead of a project team of twelve, set up three teams of four. Give each team as much autonomy as possible, with horizontal coordination between the team leads.

These approaches should be paired with policies and messaging on boundary-setting, adequate time away, and email and meeting etiquette—otherwise you could end up creating the feeling that work is ongoing at all hours, day and

---

* Just be careful that you don't overdo this. See Chapter 12 (Trust).

night. These boundaries and policies are especially important for managers, who can often struggle to support a team of employees who each have different hours or schedules.

When organizations get an employee's compensation, workload, and flexibility right, they create the Ideal Job for that employee, and the seeds of Employalty are sown.

What makes those seeds grow into something strong and healthy?

Answer: Meaningful Work.

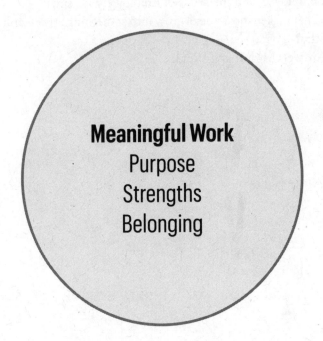

Meaningful Work
Purpose
Strengths
Belonging

MEANINGFUL WORK

8

Purpose

___

BEING A hospice chaplain involves a lot of listening and small talk. These are skills that Julie Green is still developing six months into her new job with a nursing care facility in Western Pennsylvania. "When someone is dying, they don't want to have a conversation about death, because they made that decision a while ago," she says. "So, I spend a lot of time talking about murder mysteries and the Steelers, because that's what people wanna talk about."

She needs these skills the most in the last days of someone's life. "When the nurses or aides notice that somebody is starting to transition, they ask if I can increase my visits." Julie's role is to be present for the patient and the family. "It's learning how to be an empathetic listener and following the lead of the person I go to see," she explains. "I've gotten good at holding hands and listening."

In a way, Julie is working against years of muscle memory. She is not used to long stretches of listening or idle chitchat. She's used to doing all the talking. That's because six months before taking this job as a hospice chaplain, Julie had just finished her twenty-seventh year as a college history professor. "I'd fully intended to retire from teaching at sixty-two, because my wife is older than me. I thought maybe I'd do something in ministry then, but I was always dismissive of anything pastoral." She shakes her head and smiles. "I used to joke that if I was the person standing next to your bed when you're dying, you're in trouble, and not because you're dying."

Yet here she is.

Julie's graduation from professor to pastor happened slowly and then all at once. In the last few years of her professorship, she found herself growing increasingly frustrated by what she saw as the politics and unethical practices of her university. She describes a lot of little problems that added up over time. "It was being asked to keep students eligible to play soccer or basketball. It was layoffs that didn't make sense. There were rumors about misappropriation of funds. There was a sexual harassment complaint from a student about a male professor that was poorly handled and didn't adequately protect the student." A change in the college's leadership added to Julie's growing dissatisfaction. Faculty were no longer permitted to sign student forms or approve class enrollment changes. Their schedules and workloads were no longer determined collaboratively with the registrar's office. Those who had taught at the college for years experienced a steady retraction of autonomy and creative freedom. "The administration no longer treated faculty as highly trained professionals. Our expertise wasn't valued or respected."

For years, Julie had seen her job as a simple one. "My job is to help students," she says. Near the end of her time as a professor, she no longer felt that was possible. When a close colleague resigned and said it was because she could no longer support the institution and its policies, that was a wakeup call for Julie. "It was no longer an environment where I could do my best work. I thought, *I've gotta find something else.*"

Yet it wasn't dissatisfaction alone that was affecting Julie's professional devotion. As her discontentment with the college grew, she regularly found herself thinking she was supposed to be doing something else. "I'd been attending church… and volunteering more. Each time I did more, I was encouraged and incentivized to do more. I started to think I was being called to do something but had no idea what. A bishop said, 'If you want to go to seminary, we'll pay for it.' I thought, *Wow… well… okay.* She found a program where she could continue working full-time and go to school full-time. After completing the program, Julie wasn't planning on a career change. She'd intended to keep right on working as a professor. Ministry was just how she wanted to spend her time off campus.

For a while, it worked. Outside of teaching, Julie volunteered at a federal penitentiary, leading GED classes and helping inmates with résumés. "If I had time between classes, I'd go to the prison and do a class, then come back to campus and teach my course." It wasn't long before Julie realized that she was getting professional fulfillment only from her work off campus and that the situation at the college had grown too toxic. "In my last year there, I had a long drive to campus each day and spent most of it crying," she says. "In the twenty-seven years I taught, I only ever missed two days, and one of those was for jury duty. But I noticed I started manipulating my time, like, *If I get a Covid shot on this day, I get this day off…* That's how badly I didn't want to be in that space." When she returned from a scheduled vacation, she knew she couldn't return to the college. Julie resigned.

"I quit at the college on July 16 and started my job as a chaplain on July 19."

Meaningful Work

Since the mid-1970s, a growing number of researchers have been studying the idea of Meaningful Work. What's abundantly clear in study after study is that when we perceive our work as being worthwhile, important, or valued, there is a correlating positive impact on work engagement, employee commitment, and job satisfaction. In an in-depth examination by *Entrepreneur* magazine, Michael Steger of Colorado State University said that, among other benefits, the employees engaged in Meaningful Work are more productive. "They get better supervisor ratings, they are rated as better team members, they're happy to put in discretionary work hours, and they tend to act as better brand ambassadors for their organizations." Meaningful Work also fuels retention. In one Workhuman survey, participants were asked, "What makes you stay at your company?" The top answer, given by 32 percent of respondents, was "I find the work meaningful."

While Meaningful Work is a driver of commitment, the absence of meaning in our work can accelerate disengagement and even negatively impact our health. "A lack of meaningful work has long been recognized as a primary source of alienation, anxiety, emotional exhaustion, and boredom in the modern era," according to a report published by psychologists at the University of Toronto. In other words, when Meaningful Work is present, employees stick around and give it all they've got. When it is lacking, employees spiral toward burnout. The absence of Meaningful Work results in employees simply going through the motions or leaving altogether.

Consider Julie Green's Employalty Scorecard in her last years as a college professor. It probably looked something like this:

Julie Green's Employalty Scorecard as a Professor

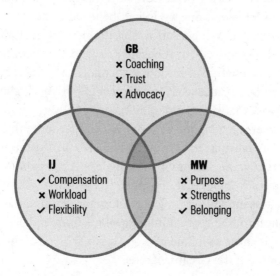

Now consider what her Employalty Scorecard looks like as hospice chaplain.

Julie Green's Employalty Scorecard as Hospice Chaplain

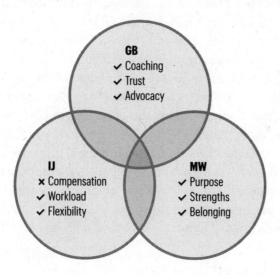

After years as a professor, Julie stopped experiencing Meaningful Work. She no longer believed in her employer. She didn't feel valued and wasn't doing work that aligned with her talents. When it became clear to her that this was the case, she left. Not for money or status. She left, as many workers do, because what was of great importance to her was to do work that she found fulfilling.

Workers are plugged in to this experience more than ever before. According to a YouGov poll, one in five American workers considers their job meaningless. A *Harvard Business Review* study found that nine out of ten workers were willing to take less money—as Julie did—for more meaningful work. The quest to find more fulfilling work is front and center for many who have switched jobs or plan to. It's one of the ongoing drivers of the Great Upgrade.

So how do we make work more meaningful?

In short, it's complicated.

What makes work meaningful varies significantly from person to person. What we each experience as meaningful is informed by our unique ambitions, values, and circumstances. Therefore, it is disingenuous to suggest that there's a singular way to cultivate Meaningful Work for all employees in an organization. That said, there are patterns and trends that have emerged, both in research and among those who change jobs, that show us the most common experiences that contribute to an employee's perception of Meaningful Work.

For one thing, we know that some employees feel more professionally fulfilled when they see that they can advance and grow in their careers. As Deloitte found in one study, loyalty is higher at companies that support employee careers and life ambitions. This is why many employers engage in proactive pay increases and title bumps as a matter of practice. The perception of forward professional momentum increases commitment. When employees perceive that there are limited or no opportunities to advance, that commitment can wane.

While upward professional mobility contributes to professional fulfillment, if you want the best chance of sparking Meaningful Work among your teams, there are three specific experiences you'll want to engineer. To harvest all the commitment that Meaningful Work creates, your organization must ensure people's jobs include purpose, strengths, and belonging. The first of these, purpose, is about what your organization stands for *and* what people believe about the impact of their work. Purpose is the foundation upon which Employalty is built.

The Power of Purpose

It's not very often that you can point to a single document released on a specific date as the moment when the rules of business were rewritten. But that's exactly what happened on August 19, 2019. That's the date the Business Roundtable (BRT) released its "Statement on the Purpose of a Corporation," which was signed by 181 American chief executives from some of the biggest companies in the world.

Since 1972, the BRT has been bringing CEOs together to share ideas, develop consensus, study issues, and formulate positions. In 1997, the organization declared unabashed adherence to economist Milton Friedman's belief that a company's only responsibility was to its shareholders. In a formal statement then, the BRT proclaimed, "The paramount duty of management and of boards of directors is to the corporation's stockholders... the interests of other stakeholders are relevant as a derivative of the duty to stockholders." That all changed two decades later when the CEOs of America's largest banks, automakers, retailers, restaurants, and tech companies declared that businesses should "share a fundamental commitment to *all* of our stakeholders," which they described to include not just shareholders, but also customers, employees, suppliers, and communities.

In their statement, these leaders declared a fundamental commitment to fair compensation and benefits along with ongoing training and education for employees. They promised to continue delivering value to customers while also dealing ethically with suppliers and supporting the communities where their employees work. They proclaimed a commitment to fostering "diversity and inclusion, dignity and respect." They stressed that this statement "supersedes previous statements and outlines a modern standard for corporate responsibility."

Upon its release, *USA Today* called the statement "stunning." Reuters called it "a bombshell." The *New York Times* said it broke "with decades of long-held corporate orthodoxy." But why did these executives publicly declare what the *Wall Street Journal* called a "major philosophical shift"?

Because it made good business sense to do so.

It turns out that standing for something beyond profits can be quite profitable. Going back three decades, two Harvard Business School professors have shown that stock prices among purposeful, values-driven companies are twelve times better over the long term. This has been driven, in part, by consumers nowadays being much more likely to spend their money on companies, products, or brands that they see as having a strong purpose. In one global study that spanned eight countries, over seventy brands, and thousands of participants, researchers found that consumers are four to six times more likely to purchase from and refer others to purpose-driven companies. But consumer behavior alone wasn't the only factor in the BRT's evolution. Purpose is also critical to attracting, retaining, and activating a capable workforce.

By 2025, Gen Z and millennial employees will make up 65 percent of the US workforce. They are already half of the world's population. Among the highest priorities and most central values of these two generations is the idea that businesses should do more than sell a product and make a profit. These generations believe that companies should meet societal needs. In an exhaustive study prior to the pandemic, Deloitte found that workers under the age of forty show deeper loyalty to employers who boldly tackle environmental and social challenges. Another study found that 81 percent of these workers expect companies to publicly pledge to be good corporate citizens. In yet a third study, 62 percent of millennials—many of whom are now your managers—indicated they would take a pay cut to work for a company that's socially responsible. Today's employees want their companies to be conscientious members of a global community.

They also want their employers to be agents of change. According to the 2022 Edelman Trust Barometer, 81 percent of employees believe their CEO should be visibly discussing with external stakeholders the work their company has done to benefit society. Go ahead and pursue corporate success, but know that to activate commitment, your workforce needs to see you protecting the planet, embracing diversity, combating poverty, respecting privacy, and acting ethically along the way.

This is where you can create a competitive advantage for your organization in the war for talent. Because, despite the high-profile signatures on the BRT's statement and the widespread coverage of its release as groundbreaking, only a handful of companies have actually made progress toward the very ideals that statement endorses. When two research-ers analyzed over six hundred documents from all 128 of the public US companies that signed on, they found only limited change had taken place to improve the treatment of stake-holders. Yet workers have never been more attuned to what companies *say* they value and whether they walk their talk. If your business can stand for something that goes beyond profit—that is, if it can articulate a mission or purpose that makes a difference in the lives of others and actively live that mission in how it operates—you will be the exception to the rule. This creates yet another distinction you can highlight to be a destination workplace in the eyes of those you recruit and employ.

Living Your Purpose

When your organization demonstrates that it is truly impact-ing lives in a positive way, you're attending to one of the essential ingredients of Employalty. What must be noted here is that *how* this impact is communicated matters. Com-panies that use generic corporate speak or focus-group-tested marketing language to describe what they do or why they exist don't seed purpose. Your organization's mission must be specific, transformational, and rooted in emotion.

When a restaurant chain declares that their mission is to be financially successful while making every guest loyal—which is the actual mission statement of one of the largest restaurant groups in the US*—they spotlight the wrong goals. Most workers aren't inspired by the idea of making money

---

*   I won't shame them publicly, but their name rhymes with *Olive Garden*.

The quest to find more fulfilling work is front and center for many who take a new job or who are tempted to leave their current one.

---

for the company or getting customers to continually return. What activates people—what leads them to believe that the daily activities in their world actually make a difference—is hearing about the impact those activities have on real people's feelings and experiences.

What's more inspiring: being told that your restaurant's mission is to "make every guest loyal" or that you're there to "create moments of relief, relaxation, and joy for stressed couples, busy friends, and tired parents"? If you worked for a CPA firm, which mission would inspire greater effort in you—"We're devoted to superior financial accuracy and outstanding client care" or "We provide business owners the comfort and peace that come with knowing that dedicated professionals are watching over their livelihoods at all times"? Which salon would you rather work for, the one whose mission is "exceptional quality, service, and style" or the one that proclaims "We help women feel confident and beautiful at their next big event"?

As you can see, purpose isn't about the product. Purpose comes from the emotion that product or service evokes in customers when it's done well. For employees to experience Meaningful Work, you need to broadcast a specific emotional purpose that makes a difference in the lives of others. This is why one of a CEO's most important roles is to define an inspiring purpose and to champion that purpose across the organization over time. To help any leader, I've included a Defining Our Purpose activity in the digital toolkit that you can download over at employaltybook.com.

But your work doesn't stop there. Your organization must live it. Where most companies fall short on purpose isn't in finding the right language (though a *lot* of mission statements need serious work). It's that they fail to live that mission in their actions. This happens when decisions aren't driven by the mission. Stories about ways the mission happens aren't shared or celebrated. Those who embody the mission are treated poorly or not retained. Leaders don't connect the daily duties of each person's job to the mission. When these actions are absent, your company doesn't have a mission, it simply has a slogan, one that's experienced by employees as an empty platitude. When they encounter it on signs or a coffee mug, they ignore it or become cynical. When these actions aren't taking place, your employees' chances to experience purpose become limited, which can then make Employalty impossible to achieve.

Here again we see direct supervisors playing a critical role. In order for your company to bring your mission to life for employees, bosses must learn how to create line of sight between the tasks and duties of each person's job and the difference that work makes in the lives of others. Let's stick with our hair salon example from above. In salons where the boss champions numbers over experiences, purpose will be lower. "Complete X number of haircuts in every shift" just doesn't feed the soul. While meeting fundamental metrics and goals is important (and must be shared with employees), the best bosses mix in stories and reminders of the specific emotional experiences the stylists can create for real people.

For example, imagine a preteen girl comes into the salon with her mother after getting a bad haircut someplace else. She's embarrassed. Distraught. She's hiding under a ballcap. On that day and with that customer, that stylist's job isn't just to give a haircut. It's to help that young person overcome the agony of her social discomfort. The stylist's job is to be the caring surrogate aunt who says, "We got this. I'm going to take good care of you, and you're gonna walk out of here loving your new look, okay?" At this, you can almost see the relief flood the girl's face, right? Her shoulders relax.

She settles into the chair. Her mother says a silent prayer in thanks for this stylist who *gets it* and said exactly what her daughter needed to hear.* If I'm the salon manager, these are the reminders and stories I'm constantly sharing with my team members to cultivate purpose and nurture Meaningful Work.

This action—managers consistently articulating how employees' work contributes to the mission—is among the most important in this book. Triggering purpose comes from each individual employee being able to personalize their impact, which leads to employees taking more ownership of their work and their role in the organization. When bosses help employees see and hear the ways that their unique contributions make your mission happen, they ultimately believe not just that "*my company* makes a difference" but that "*I* make a difference."

The impact of this kind of boss behavior is observable. In a large study of more than four hundred US companies, researchers found that employers whose managers excel in mission-connected communication have systemically better financial performance than their peers. In another study, just a 10 percent improvement in employees' connection with the mission or purpose of their organization led to decreases in turnover and increases in profitability.

Here again we see the power of Employalty. When workers believe that what they do matters, they stay longer and do work that is higher in quality.

---

* If this sounds like a uniquely specific example, it is. This happened to my eleven-year-old daughter. We call that story "When pixie cuts go wrong."

You Better Recognize

Another crucial tactic for fostering purpose is creating a culture of ongoing recognition. When employees are celebrated for their contributions, they experience purpose and, thus, Meaningful Work. Scores of studies have demonstrated the crucial role recognition plays in motivating and retaining workers. Recently the Great Place to Work organization analyzed 1.7 million employee survey responses from companies of all sizes to determine the most important drivers of great work. Recognition was, far and away, the top answer given: A notable 37 percent of respondents said that more personal recognition would encourage them to produce better work more often. In another report, 69 percent of employees indicated they would work harder if they felt their efforts were better appreciated.

Most companies and leaders know this. It's why recognition is a $46 billion a year industry. What most companies and leaders get wrong, though, is the most effective kind of recognition. Of the recognition programs that employers use, 87 percent focus on tenure. That is to say, the most common type of recognition in the workplace—by a mile—is celebrating years of service. While celebrating *time* isn't *bad*, as the primary method for acknowledging contributions, it leaves much to be desired. For one thing, it means many employees go an entire year without recognition; in companies that only acknowledge more formal milestones—five, ten, or twenty years, for example—and do nothing else, recognition is practically nonexistent. For another, celebrating tenure doesn't celebrate a person's unique talents or contributions. You're only praising that they are still there. In this way, that employee is no different than the coffee maker that is also still there and still working. To truly leverage the power of recognition, stop recognizing people just for showing up. Instead, spotlight *how* they show up.

If you want people to believe they are valued and appreciated, you must explicitly state what it is they do or have done that has made a difference. "Thank you" doesn't go far enough. "Thank you for being so patient with that disgruntled customer" is much more powerful, as it zeroes in on the specific talent or action the employee brought to bear on their work in the moment. Telling someone "You're a valued member of the team" is nice, but we supercharge it when we say, "You're a valued member of the team for a lot of reasons, but especially because you always keep everyone calm and positive when we're understaffed and overbooked." When we hear about the unique contributions we make, we feel truly valued. We have purpose. One study on motivation found that praise from your direct boss is more motivating than performance-based cash bonuses.

This is the primary aspect of effective recognition that many employers get wrong. They focus on a present, like gift cards or company swag. Attach gifts to your efforts if you want, but it's not the gift that matters, it's the sentiment inside the card that's attached to the gift. At a workshop recently, a manager told me that she wants her team to feel appreciated. She then said, "I buy pizza, I give out candy, I make certificates... I'm running out of ideas." I encouraged her to abandon the giveaways. I told her to take fifteen minutes each week to write a couple of sincere sticky notes, thank you cards, or emails to team members describing one thing about them she was grateful for. Less than a month later, she emailed me. "I can't believe how deeply moved people have been by these little notes I started leaving. I wish I would have started years ago. I could've made people feel even more appreciated while saving a ton of money on pizza."

This is why, when I'm asked to recommend the most effective type of employee recognition programs, I focus on communication. Stop trying to create the right award or structure or points system. The very best recognition "programs" are those that trigger a manager or peer to directly acknowledge a specific and timely talent or contribution that someone made. It really is that simple. What matters is that it's not rare. Some researchers have suggested that recognition has a "shelf life" of about one week. However much you're doing, you should probably do more.

Notice that I included the word "peer" above. A recognition culture doesn't just place the onus for celebrating others solely on the manager (though they play an important role). At companies getting this right, there is a shared responsibility across the team for engaging in recognition regularly. Manager-to-employee recognition is certainly the most important kind, but peer recognition can be just as powerful at helping employees feel valued and, therefore, experience purpose. A few years back, SHRM found that peer-to-peer recognition is nearly 36 percent more likely to have a positive impact on financial results than manager-only recognition. So make time at your next team meeting for members to spotlight the contributions of others. Equip people with certificates or stickers or a bulletin board to thank teammates or celebrate their difference-making.

Remember, one of the primary ways people experience purpose—and therefore Meaningful Work—is when they believe their work positively impacts the lives of others. In this case "others" can (and should) include co-workers. Seeing that what I do is of value to and appreciated by my co-workers can check that same emotional and psychological box as seeing that something I did on the job mattered to a customer or supervisor.

But purpose alone doesn't create Meaningful Work. There is a key second ingredient that must be present for employees to experience the professional fulfillment that activates commitment. On a consistent basis, employees must get to do work that aligns with their strengths.

9

Strengths

———

THIRTY APPLICANTS in twenty-four hours. That's how Jessica Young knew the team was on to something.

Jessica is the Senior Director for Inclusion and Learning at Reliant Medical Group, a primary and specialty care provider in Central Massachusetts. Reliant has more than five hundred providers in over thirty specialties serving 300,000 patients. In 2021, their front desk operations were precariously understaffed. "At one point we had thirty-five openings for these roles and a retention rate of just 80 percent. We knew we had to do something."

Front-line clinical staff—or "Patient Service Specialists," as they are called at Reliant—are critical to healthcare operations, and the work isn't easy. "Being a PSS is challenging and is growing more complex," Jessica noted. These are the employees who book appointments and check people in. They need to understand medical terminology and insurance. They have to move around in a variety of software programs. They must be adept at customer service. "Any provider in my organization will tell you that if they lose a really good PSS, it impacts patient care." Jessica was part of a small team at Reliant tasked with figuring out how to improve recruitment and retention in these vital front-line roles. She said that, early on, they realized they would need a multiprong strategy. "There is no one thing... we had to implement a whole lotta things."

Eventually, they sought and received executive approval for a three-phase plan that focused on recruiting differently, increasing new-hire training, and creating a more inclusive culture that, among other things, offered more flexible positions. "We started by asking, 'Who is our audience? What do they need?' This is an entry-level role that doesn't require licensure or certification, or a degree, or taking a test, as most positions in healthcare do. We realized that there are a lot of people who want to work in healthcare who just don't know how to get in, and that's what we can offer." Jessica's team also agreed that at the foundation of the position was customer service. "We wanted people who could treat our patients and our other employees with care. It really came down to a passion for helping people. Everything else we can teach."

When the team looked at the job posting used to recruit candidates for the PSS positions, they realized they were limiting themselves. Jessica laughs at the memory. "We just kicked ourselves. No wonder it wasn't working." Here's how Reliant previously recruited their front desk workers:

Qualifications:

- high school diploma

- additional specialized medical secretary or medical office training preferred

- superior customer service skills

- ability to think critically

- excellent communication, interpersonal, and organizational skills

- familiarity with various software applications such as Microsoft Office, etc.

"There are a lot of unnecessary requirements on there that will turn individuals away," Jessica told me. "Research actually shows that most women won't apply for a position if they don't meet most or all of the qualifications, whereas men will apply if they only meet one or two. So we just took it all away. You don't need a high school diploma. You don't need prior medical secretary experience or Microsoft Office skills. We changed it all out. We decided that if you want to work here, we'll train you to do it. Just come here and be awesome."

After revising the qualifications list for the position, the team posted a new job ad. In twenty-four hours, it generated thirty applications, more than Reliant had ever received for the PSS role in a one-day period. Here's how they list the qualifications for the position now:

The ideal applicant is highly motivated, has a great attitude, and a strong desire to work in a healthcare setting where they can make a positive impact.

No medical office experience required; we will train you.

Join our Reliant Medical Group team today!

Once they got the job posting fixed, Jessica's team sought out partnerships with schools and agencies to help them fill positions. "Most of the time, it's post and pray," she said. "We wanted to rethink traditional recruitment." They partnered with GED programs, vocational schools, criminal justice re-entry programs, disability services, and refugee relocation programs. With these partnerships and over a period of just a few months, Reliant Medical Group generated a tenfold increase in applicants to their PSS positions.

Jessica's team knew, however, that effective recruitment wouldn't be enough. "There will be a skills gap, because they have never worked in healthcare before, so we developed a twelve-week training program." This was the focus of phase two of the team's plan: create a learning culture that allows a cohort of candidates to be hired into the organization prior to position placement. "We made the decision to make it a paid training program. We felt like if we committed to them, they would commit back to us. So we have them all come in at a base rate. What's really neat for them is at the end of the twelve-week program, most of them had a pay raise already because by then we consider them skilled. So that's a huge win off the bat for them."

Over the twelve-week program, the new hires train on professionalism and accountability. They get training on keyboarding and business writing, medical terminology, and basics of insurance, billing, and coding. They also spend time learning about time management, critical thinking, and even interviewing skills. "We overlook things during the interview because, I'll be honest, a lot of them wouldn't be hired by a traditional manager. So if they show up in jeans or walk in carrying a drink, it doesn't bother us. We're like, 'That's trainable... we can teach or coach around that after we get them through the door.'"

The training program also includes job shadowing. One day a week, each person in the cohort spends an entire day with a department. This gives them a chance to see the real-world work they'll be doing and allows them to explore where they might want to work when they complete the training program. Jessica says it's a chance to connect their interests with a department that meets them. "For example, we had one woman who came back after going to the surgery desk in neurology and she said, 'That's the coolest department ever! I don't know what I'm gonna do if I can't work there.' She never even knew she liked that until she had that exposure."

Once the new hires complete the training phase, Jessica says they can match to a location. "Many of the individuals in our last cohort got up to five different offers from different areas. We had managers sweating, like, 'I really hope she picks me.'" After these candidates get placed, Jessica says they stay. "Everyone is still here that's been through a cohort. We've not had one person leave our organization." In addition to retaining staff who have been uniquely prepared to work in their organization, Reliant's approach has dramatically cut down on the time it takes to fill a position with a qualified candidate. "Our time-to-fill average went from forty-eight days to fourteen days for the PSS position," Jessica says. Now when a PSS at Reliant decides to move up or move on, "a manager can say, 'Where's the cohort at, I want to hire right from it.'"

"What's really interesting," Jessica tells me, "Is that we're now talking about this [approach] as our standard of hire. Forget about just putting postings out there to hire. We are seeing the impact of bringing someone in, training them up the way that we are, and then placing them." To continue attracting and retaining a diverse pool of candidates, Jessica's team deployed a third phase to their approach, which focuses on flexibility and career pathing. "We're working on more part-time and job share options, flexible options, and remote work as well. It's a huge culture shift for us." But Reliant is taking this action because they know what many other organizations now know: that offering more flexibility on when, where, and how people work is key to retention. So, too, are clear opportunities for ambitious people to progress. "We also now have five levels of Patient Service Specialist, so you can be a PSS 1, a PSS 2, and then you can move to a lead 1, lead 2, and then supervisor," Jessica says.

Think about all the aspects of the three-phase program Jessica's team created and executed. Without even realizing it, the team at Reliant Medical Group seeded nearly all the ingredients for Employalty among their PSS cohorts. New hires experience all the dimensions of their Ideal Job early on by being given a base pay with the chance for it to grow (compensation), being brought along slowly (workload), and having flexibility on when, where, and how they work. These new hires also immediately get to work with program directors and instructors who act as Great Bosses, granting trust and engaging in coaching and advocacy from the first day. These new hires also experience Meaningful Work by seeing quickly how much they matter to the organization (purpose) and how they fit into a team or department (belonging).

But more than anything else, what Reliant Medical Group did was spark commitment by focusing on strengths. They desperately needed to attract and retain a specific kind of employee for a challenging role in a marketplace that wasn't flooded with available candidates. Jessica's team started with something elemental: a desire to work in healthcare and deliver outstanding customer service. These traits, they decided, were the core strengths necessary for a person to be successful at the job *and* be likely to stay in the role. It is this approach that is at the heart of their success. They acted on something that social science researchers have gotten clearer and clearer on in recent years: getting to do work that aligns with our strengths is a powerful driver of Meaningful Work.

Only the Strong Thrive

Strengths are the habits, talents, and skills that we do both well and easily. For example, some people are gifted at negotiation or de-escalating agitated customers. Some of us have a knack for organizing information or creating detailed plans. Some display a talent for more creative pursuits like design or writing or performing. Our strengths aren't just the things we're good at. In most cases, they also bring us enjoyment. We tend to like doing what we're good at. When we get to use our various gifts for long stretches of time, it can lead to intense concentration and productivity. If you've ever gotten lost in a task or a project—losing all track of time while simultaneously being energized and highly focused—this could be a sign that you were using your strengths.

This feeling of being "in the zone" has a name. It's called a flow state.* When we experience flow, we've landed in a psychological sweet spot that capitalizes on our knowledge, gifts, and experience in a kind of perfect ratio. What we're working on isn't too hard, but it isn't too easy either. It's just right. Neuroscientists have shown that getting to use our strengths in this way can produce a dopamine response in the brain, leading to feelings of pleasure and motivation. Flow experiences also go a long way to preventing burnout in the workplace.

Despite a significant body of research (more on that in a moment) that suggests orienting a person's job to their strengths can produce desirable results, many organizations take employee strengths for granted. Instead, leaders have traditionally emphasized improving deficits. It's far more

---

*   As opposed to when we mindlessly scroll on our smartphones, which could most accurately be described as a zombie state.

Investing in people's
strengths has proven
to be a far more effective
path to commitment
at work than managing
weaknesses.

_____

common for employees to be asked to grow in the areas of their greatest weaknesses than to zero in on their gifts or talents. In this way, companies are chasing across-the-board mediocrity over calculated, targeted excellence. Put simply, when we spend most of our time laboring to improve what we're not good at and don't enjoy, motivation decreases. While minimizing weaknesses can prevent failure, research suggests that it cannot inspire excellence. In the most exhaustive literature review ever conducted on strengths use in the workplace, one outcome was demonstrably clear: investing in people's strengths is a far more effective path to commitment at work than managing weaknesses.

Let's consider a thirty-four-year-old woman in the role of Executive Assistant to the Chief Operating Officer of a manufacturing company. Her name is Aaliyah. After two years on the job, Aaliyah has demonstrated a real talent for creativity and design. While managing the executive's calendar, communications, and assorted projects, she's also created stunning newsletters, slide decks, signage, and webpages. Aaliyah enthusiastically describes this work as her favorite part of her job. At the same time, she struggles to remember the names and responsibilities of the various colleagues, clients, and vendor partners the COO convenes with regularly. As the gatekeeper to the busy executive, there are a lot of people to keep straight and doing this well has not come easily to her. Overall, Aaliyah is seen as competent at her job by her boss, but they both know that two years in, she should probably be faster at some of her duties. In most places, there would be an expectation that Aaliyah work to improve her competence in her area of greatest weakness. She'd be expected to get better and faster at knowing who's who. She might even receive a below average rating in some areas on an annual performance review, minimizing or altogether preventing a merit-based pay increase until such improvement occurs.

A case can be made that Aaliyah *and* the company will benefit significantly by finding a way for her to use her strengths more often, rather than devoting time to improving her weaknesses. A strengths-based approach to employee experience would see the organization move her into a full-time role that allows her to do the design work she's gifted at more often while minimizing the people-tracking that isn't her strength. Perhaps she can fill an opening on the marketing team. Maybe a new role gets created for her inside a department or in the C-suite. However this evolution occurs, the research is clear. Once Aaliyah gets to use her strengths more frequently, both she and her employer will benefit in myriad ways.

Employees who are actively encouraged to use their strengths at work handle their workload more effectively, show lower levels of absenteeism, and describe higher job satisfaction. They also experience more flow, vitality, and energy on the job and report higher overall well-being outside of work. There is a correlation between these outcomes and the amount of time employees get to operate from their strengths. The more hours a day adults believe they use their strengths, the more they report having ample energy, feeling well-rested, being happy, smiling or laughing a lot, learning something interesting, and being treated with respect. Employees who get to use their strengths every day are three times as likely to report having an excellent quality of life and six times as likely to be engaged at work. As a result, organizations that prioritize employee strengths see a wide array of measurable benefits.

Back in 2016, Gallup completed the most extensive study of workgroups using strengths-based interventions ever conducted. Across fifty thousand business units with 1.2 million employees in forty-five countries, prioritizing strengths produced profound results. In workgroups where employees said their manager focused on strengths, 70 percent of employees were engaged. In groups where managers didn't focus on strengths, the percentage of engaged workers was a staggering 2 percent.

Even more stunningly, 90 percent of the workgroups using strengths-based interventions had increases in sales, profit, customer satisfaction, and employee engagement.

In the case of Aaliyah, increasing the amount of time she spends doing the work that most aligns with her strengths is a clear path to Meaningful Work. What's worth noting is that this would still be the case even if Aaliyah had no gaps in her performance as an Executive Assistant. Even if she easily remembered names and details and demonstrated a high degree of competence in all aspects of her EA role, the company and the employee will both reap greater long-term benefits by engineering a way for Aaliyah to do more of what she's most gifted at.

This is how we move away from trying to find the best person for the job and instead create the best *job* for the *person*. This is the mutual commitment that is at the heart of Employalty. Unfortunately, what happens at too many places is that the employee never imagines they could try their hand at a different kind of position. Or they are prevented from doing so, which is a recipe for disengagement and turnover. If Aaliyah applies for and is offered a design job only to have the COO intervene because he doesn't want to endure training a replacement, Aaliyah's commitment is as good as gone. As I outlined in the chapter on dehumanization, there's almost no coming back from this. Aaliyah will likely quit because she has learned that her boss sees her as a commodity to be retained for his convenience, not a human being with dreams, needs, and agency.

Getting Started with Strengths

Giving employees the chance to explore their interests, identify their gifts, and then consistently use their strengths is a
critical component of Meaningful Work.* To implement a
strengths-based approach to the employee experience in your
organization, start by introducing the concept to managers
and employees. Consider a tool like CliftonStrengths, the
VIA Survey of Character Strengths, or the Strengths Profile,
all accessible online. These are reputable, evidence-based
assessments that can help individuals identify and articulate
their strengths. Also, create systems that encourage managers to notice employee strengths and discuss them with their
direct reports regularly. This can take place as part of recur-
ring one-on-one meetings, annual reviews, or quarterly "stay
interviews," in which managers periodically check in with
employees about why they stay and what would cause them
to leave.† (A sample stay interview can be found in the free
digital toolkit for this book, available at employaltybook.com.)

Through observation and conversation about what managers see and what employees tell us they enjoy or believe
they are good at, you can then take steps to increase the use
of these strengths in their day-to-day work. Have someone
who has a talent for staying calm in times of chaos? Ask them
to share tips or insights at an upcoming team meeting. Maybe
that turns into a formal piece of training that becomes a part

---

*   Remember Jack Merrill, who created more flexibility for his hospital
     HVAC team? His pilot program ended up creating opportunities for
     employees to try different job duties. While piloting flexibility, Jack
     inadvertently allowed employees to also work to their strengths. This
     is a part of the reason his program was so successful.

†   As opposed to exit interviews, which are a waste of time. See *Boss
     Better Now* podcast episode #23.

of your new-hire orientation. Is there a member of your sales team who showcases a capacity for networking far more effectively than what other sales professionals in the organization demonstrate? Perhaps she would enjoy mentoring others who desire to improve in this area.

But you can't let this observation and conversation slide for long periods of time because, let's remember, our strengths change over the course of our lives. What we're good at and what we find interesting fluctuates and can develop continuously with the passage of time. After all, we are different at age sixty-two from who we were at age forty-two, let alone at age twenty-two. For this reason, conversations about aligning employee strengths to job roles should be an ongoing practice.

While these regular conversations are important, it is not enough to just notice and acknowledge strengths. As leaders, we must install ways for our team members to utilize their gifts. This requires intentionality on the part of the leader and adaptability on the part of the organization. Eschew the belief that, as job roles go, one size fits all. Every person on your team is a unique individual. Some aspects of their job duties can be unique as well, to create alignment between that person's talents and their ongoing job responsibilities. This is a practice that is often referred to as "job crafting," where leaders and employees work hand-in-hand to design a person's role exclusively around their gifts and interests. In some organizations, and for some leaders specifically, this will require a mindset shift. It can be hard to let go of the notion that the job *description* determines a person's job *duties*. But to create Meaningful Work, here again, we're working to create the best *job* for the *person*, not the other way around.

Part of this mindset shift is accepting that strengths are an intrinsic part of human nature. Every employee is inherently good at *something*. It's the leader's job to get clear on what that might be and then increase that person's opportunities to engage with those talents. There will be times when this will require the organization to adjust a position or move the employee to an altogether new role. While the logistics may feel burdensome at times, as outlined above, the return on investment can be significant. Only when the employee has proven incapable of effectively deploying their strengths or unwilling to do so with a commitment to quality or in accordance with company expectations do we then decide that perhaps they are not the right fit for the organization.

Likewise, prioritizing strengths means we must periodically challenge conventional thinking on who is the right fit for a job role or promotion. This is what Reliant Medical Group did. In some organizations, technical expertise or years of experience are granted outsized weight when, in many cases, it is strengths that should be given heaviest consideration. Consider how we've long determined who gets promoted to a supervisor role. Most managers were promoted because of their experience or expertise. They were, for example, the best financial analyst, so they got tapped to lead a team of financial analysts. As you will learn in upcoming pages, this is one of the most common errors we make when it comes to choosing who to name "boss." What we should be doing to identify leaders is focus less on technical expertise and more on strengths. When we see someone in possession of the skills and habits that make for strong leaders—building trust, relationships, coaching others, and communication, to name a few—there stands in front of us a potential candidate for a future leadership role because they demonstrate many of the strengths that role requires, even if they lack the experience or technical expertise of those they'll oversee.

As part of your journey to more intentionally align people's work with their talents, it's also important that team members become aware of each other's strengths. There is research that suggests that when strengths are recognized by close others, teams can share and celebrate accomplishments and work together more effectively, both of which further contribute to Meaningful Work. This also means that, as leaders, we are thoughtful about strengths when assembling teams, committees, or project groups. It's important to create a diversity of ability across a group of people charged to work together and to ensure that the various talents people bring to a working group complement and balance one another.

This is one way a tool like CliftonStrengths can be highly useful. It gives everyone on the team a vocabulary they can use to name and understand each person's unique gifts. Possessing such insight then empowers everyone on the team to play to and ultimately appreciate each other's strengths. In this way, there's a connection between strengths and purpose. When an employee gets to operate from the locus of their gifts and talents, they don't just become more effective, they more frequently experience feeling valued. When we get to do what we do well, it's much more common for us to experience recognition and appreciation for what we bring to the organization, both via our supervisors and teammates. Focusing on strengths, it would seem, is yet another strategy for supercharging purpose, and therefore, Meaningful Work.

In fact, teams play a significant role in whether an employee experiences Meaningful Work. What we know is that, in addition to purpose and strengths, employees derive fulfillment—and therefore commitment—from one more set of experiences that is central to feelings of Meaningful Work. It's a set of experiences that we'll capture in a single word: belonging.

10

Belonging

JEREMY SCHMIDT is the Director of Global Talent for Codility, a technical recruiting platform that helps companies make evidence-based hiring decisions. Or, as Jeremy describes it, "We remove a lot of the unconscious bias that we all know exists on the HR and talent side" around hiring software engineers.

Both by the nature of his role and the mission of his company, it is Jeremy's job to know what attracts other people to jobs. "How quickly things have changed in just a short amount of time is mind-blowing to me," Jeremy told me. "Five years ago, if you offer someone five grand more, they're probably going to change jobs. And what we've seen now is a complete shift. People have had a lot of time to really think about what's important to them. They've figured out that working somewhere that has a vision and mission they can get behind and where they're treated like adults means more to them than just the $5,000 raise."

It's Jeremy's job to compete for talent in a global marketplace. What's more important now than ever before? "The companies that are attracting talent show an empathetic and compassionate culture. And it isn't just a bunch of fluff like, 'Hey, we have mental health days.' Employers have to put some substance behind that and articulate it as a process." What kind of substance? "One of the things I get asked about the most is how people are supported from a cultural perspective. People want to be treated fairly and equitably and be able to bring their true selves to work. We need to embrace that. We need to create an environment where everyone can feel 150 percent comfortable to be their authentic selves."

Jeremy is right. According to a study from employee review site Glassdoor, 76 percent of employees and job seekers said a diverse workforce was important when evaluating companies and job offers. Another study by one of the world's largest consulting firms put that number at 80 percent. Online, job seekers are being transparent about their quest for an employer that demonstrates an ongoing commitment to, among other things, diversity, equity, and inclusion (DEI). It's not uncommon for candidates to ask about diverse hiring processes and the presence of unconscious bias training. They're also looking at the makeup of the leadership group and the team they'd be joining and, for larger companies, checking to see if there is a Chief DEI officer. Many candidates check sites like Glassdoor to see if negative reviews have been posted about a company by people from underrepresented groups.

The executive team at Codility knows that embracing an empathetic, welcoming culture for all employees requires more than just vocal support for these ideals. It requires visible, consistent action over time at all levels of the organization. At Codility, this starts with hiring. "We drive diversity and innovation by sourcing top-of-the-funnel candidates that are going to help us change in the right ways, where we can all learn together," Jeremy says.

Another commitment Codility makes is their ongoing support of employee resource groups (ERGs). ERGs are employee-led groups that endeavor to make workplaces safer and more supportive for employees who share a characteristic, ethnicity, experience, or interest. When ERGs are actively supported by senior leadership, they can improve work conditions, facilitate open conversations, develop leaders, and bring frustrations to the surface quickly and safely.

ERGs have grown in popularity in recent years. They can be found in 90 percent of Fortune 500 companies. They're also present in many organizations that win great-place-to-work designations. At Codility, five ERGs are supported and funded by the organization: an LGBTQ group, a families group, a women-in-tech group, a neuro-diverse employees group, and a group for people of color. Each group is employee-led, has a budget provided by the organization, and enjoys a direct line of communication with senior leadership.

Jeremy has seen first-hand the impact ERGs can have. The women's ERG, for example, helps hold the organization accountable for gender diversity in hiring. "We provide them [with information on] how many women were in the final discussions for any director's level role, how many women we hire compared to men, etc. We talk a lot about those things to find areas where we could be making mistakes so we can get better." Employee resource groups can also drive continuing education and cultural competence. "Our LGBTQ group had four of our employees volunteer to do a company webinar about their coming out experience, how they identify, and why pronouns matter. For a company that has a lot of white males in the Eastern Bloc of Europe, it changes people's perception. For someone that has bias out there, people are listening and maybe thinking a little bit differently. They didn't have to put themselves out there, but everybody on the panel said, 'I've never worked at a company where I felt more comfortable talking about these things.'"

ERG groups don't just exist to drive inclusive cultures. They can also impact morale and a sense of mattering. "Our families ERG had some extra money in the budget so, as a surprise, they sent $50 DoorDash credits to everyone in that ERG near the end of the year," Jeremy recalls. "They said, 'The holidays can be stressful, so don't worry about cooking dinner tonight.' That's just another little thing that someone gets and thinks, *Holy cow, look what they do here*. It goes a long way."

For ERGs to work in an organization, they can't just exist on paper. At Codility, their groups are a top priority. Every ERG has a private Slack channel for interaction. They each meet with the Chief People Officer quarterly to work on initiatives. All job candidates are given the chance to speak with a member of an ERG group in the company as part of the interview process. "A lot of companies create ERGs, but they fall to the wayside," Jeremy says. "We pull data from [these groups], track it, and show the areas where we're getting better. We also make sure we have someone amazing driving these initiatives." What Codility is doing with their ERGs mirrors what organizations of all shapes and sizes have leaned in to in recent years, because of what we've learned about why employees join, stay with, or leave an employer.

Among the most important factors is whether employees can emphatically say, "I belong here."

The Rise of Belonging

Global consulting firm Deloitte has been conducting and compiling research on human resources, talent, and workplace trends for more than a decade. Theirs is a body of work that represents some of the longest-running and most comprehensive studies on these topics ever conducted. Upon the release of their 2021 Global Human Capital Trends* report, one trend stood out more than any other: the influence of *belonging* at work. Deloitte's researchers define "belonging" as workers feeling *comfortable* at work, including being treated fairly and respected by colleagues, feeling *connected* to the people they work with and the teams they are a part of, and feeling that they *contribute* to meaningful work outcomes. They describe belonging as one of the most important issues for attracting, retaining, and activating employees in today's workplace.

This is backed up by employee feedback and research across the globe. McKinsey found that a lack of belonging is one of the top three reasons people quit a job post-pandemic, with 51 percent of employees citing it as the primary reason they left. Nearly as many workers cited the desire to find an environment where they can "work with people who trust and care for each other." As McKinsey put it, employees want stronger relationships, a sense of connection, and to be seen. In a global study from Cognizant, 92 percent of respondents said it was important to "feel like you are appreciated for who you are and what you can contribute," and 62 percent said belonging was more important than salary. Indeed's 2021 Work Happiness Score research revealed that belonging is the top driver of well-being for employees and an essential driver of happiness at work, ranking higher than pay.

Belonging doesn't just lead people to stay. It's part of the cocktail of conditions organizations must foster to drive employee engagement, and thus higher performance. In 2019, the *Harvard Business Review* published an article titled "The Value of Belonging at Work." The researchers found that just one incident of exclusion can lead to an immediate 25 percent

---

* That name, though. Yuck.

decline in an individual's performance on a team project. Yet, when companies get belonging right, workers produce demonstrably better results. In the same study, belonging was linked to a 56 percent increase in job performance, a 50 percent drop in turnover risk, and a 75 percent reduction in sick days. In a separate publication—the 2022 Workplace Belonging Survey—nearly all employees (88 percent) at the companies surveyed agreed that a sense of belonging led to higher productivity at work. From a cost perspective, a focus on belonging could result in annual savings of over $52 million for a ten-thousand-person company.

"Belonging is not a program or initiative, it is an experience related to social connectedness, feeling included, and being accepted," said Dr. Rumeet Billan, who commissioned the Workplace Belonging Survey. "It's not just about inviting everyone to the proverbial table. What happens when they get there? Now, more than ever, companies and employers must take a more human-centered approach to how they support, communicate, and engage with their employees."

The proliferation of research that shows the impact that the absence or presence of belonging can have on employees has made one thing clear: employers of all sizes must attend to belonging to remain viable. Doing so is a foundational component of becoming a destination workplace. To explore the strategies and tactics organizations must embrace to nurture belonging, we'll use the very framework provided by our earlier definition of the term: comfort, connection, and contribution.

Making Workplaces Comfortable for All

Belonging has proven to be such an integral part of the employee experience that in recent years the letter "B" has been added to the commonly used DEI acronym. Diversity, equity, inclusion, and belonging (DEIB) describes the broad efforts, policies, and strategies organizations use to ensure each team member has equal opportunities to do their best work and feel valued.* To increase belonging in the workplace, organizations must work to make all employees feel comfortable.

Resist the temptation to apply a casual definition of the word "comfortable" to what you should endeavor to create for your teams. For our purposes, "comfortable" doesn't mean the absence of stress or that work should never be anything but easy. When we discuss making workplaces comfortable for all, we're attempting to create an environment where employees don't experience *exclusion*. That is to say, we must work to prevent employees from feeling marginalized or disqualified for who they are. Organizations that establish this kind of culture are twice as likely to meet or exceed financial targets, three times as likely to be high-performing, six times as likely to be innovative and agile, and eight times as likely to achieve better business outcomes.

Dr. Shirley Davis has worked as the Chief Diversity and Inclusion Officer for several Fortune 100 companies and was previously the VP of Global Diversity and Inclusion and Workforce Strategies for the Society for Human Resource Management (SHRM). She's worked with organizations in more than thirty countries and most recently was tapped to write the first-ever *Diversity, Equity, & Inclusion for Dummies* book. Dr. Davis says that reducing exclusion starts with

---

*   Each word in the acronym means something different and exploring each concept in greater depth is a worthwhile investment of time for any leader. For now, we'll simply say that diversity is about representation, equity is about opportunity, inclusion is about value, and belonging is an experience.

education. "If you haven't had some level of training or development or coaching on this, that's the first thing. Leaders have to bring teams together—teams that have a diversity of perspectives, ideas, and ways of working—so they can better serve their customers and communities." Training for both leaders and team members is key. "Team members need to be able to not only work from the way they see the world, but also to understand and lead from another person's perspective as well. You're not vacating who you are or your own identity, beliefs, and values. You're recognizing that your way is not the only way of seeing the world and working with people."

In addition to education, leaders must create psychological safety. This term refers to the belief that one will not be punished or humiliated for speaking up with ideas, questions, concerns, or mistakes. One benefit of psychological safety is that it allows teams to open a dialogue—which at times can be awkward and uncomfortable—about the different backgrounds, experiences, beliefs, and needs people have. "We haven't always given people the permission to even talk about these tough and uncomfortable conversations," Dr. Davis says, "but you've got to have an environment that allows people to feel safe and share their stories." From there, Dr. Davis encourages leaders to model inclusive micro-behaviors that prioritize curiosity over judgment when learning about people or to explore differences. "It's about listening, asking questions, and being curious about the way people think, work, and believe, and not being quick to pass judgment. But also, look for common ground and shared meaning. There's something you have in common with every single person you come into contact with."

In the long run, the goal is to foster the kind of environment that celebrates the differences we bring to the workplace. One of the biggest obstacles to nurturing this

Employees are abandoning noxious cultures of competition, exclusion, gossip, infighting, and tribalism.

---

kind of culture is team members who would sabotage belonging. It's not uncommon to discover—among organizations whose employees report the absence of belonging—that someone on the team could be described as toxic. This person engages in back-channel communications, public or private criticism, cliques, keeping score, demeaning or dismissive comments, and pitting people against each other, among other troublesome behaviors. Because of how they show up, they're not just sabotaging belonging, they're sabotaging the engagement of your entire workforce, the results they are there to produce, and, therefore, the mission and stability of your organization.

If this list of behaviors made you think of a specific employee where you work, that's an obvious sign that there's a toxic presence sabotaging belonging on your team. If that's the case, one thing is clear: they must change or go. Don't fall into the trap of believing that the good things they bring to your organization—like experience or a specific skill set—outweigh the damage they inflict. That's almost never the case. When organizations approach me about doing staff development work or team retreats because of a lot of team drama, I always ask this question: "Is there one person on the team, or maybe two, who by leaving today and never coming back would make most of these problems go away?" The answer is always yes. That's when I ask a second question (gently, of course): "So your employees, culture, and performance have been suffering for months (usually years), costing you who-knows-how-much in lost time, productivity, and retention, and now you're about to spend tens of thousands of dollars on training and consulting to try and fix what they've caused. Do you mind me asking... Why is this person still there?"

There's almost never a satisfactory answer that justifies the circumstances.

Making Connections between People

Research clearly shows that diverse teams drive more revenue, make better decisions, catch more errors, and innovate
more often. But a mix of backgrounds or identities alone
won't propel diverse teams to high levels of performance.
Team members must feel connected to the people they work
with. The employee resource groups that Codility and other
companies have installed are one powerful way to enhance
connection and, ultimately, belonging. Groups aimed at
connecting people with similar backgrounds and identities
have been shown to promote stronger connections among
employees. They work because they create communities
within companies, where people can more easily build the
kinds of sophisticated relationships that belonging requires.
At a minimum, employers must take a step back and look at
their overall makeup to see whether members of their organization are more or less likely to find co-workers of similar
background, identity, or experience on the job.

As Jeremy Schmidt described above, sourcing a diversity
of talent is a part of building a work community that makes
connection for all people more possible. In places where the
gender, ethnic, racial, ability, or identity makeup is homog-
enous, those from underrepresented groups are likely to
struggle to experience belonging. In other words, if I look
around my place of employment and don't see others like
me, I may struggle to experience the comfort and connection
that belonging requires. We see these experiences reported
in much of the research that is ongoing about retention.
The Workplace Belonging Survey revealed that one in four
women reported feeling lonely at work. As part of that survey, participants were asked what they wished their peers and
colleagues knew about stressors that were impacting their day-
to-day life at work. One survey respondent said, "It's hard

Connection
occurs when
employees
build meaningful
relationships
with co-workers
over time.

———————

being the only woman and person of color in my position." Another pointed out "how hard it is to be a younger female in a predominantly older male community."

Connection also occurs when employees build meaningful relationships with co-workers over time. This experience doesn't come from potlucks and fun-based teambuilding alone, though these are important activities to nurture camaraderie and reduce team drama, as I wrote about at length in my previous book.* Connection occurs when team members form more sophisticated relationships with one another. Such relationships begin to take hold when teammates find things in common that have little to do with work. When teammates see each other not just as the person responsible for a certain set of tasks or duties at work, but as a whole person with a life, interests, and meaningful relationships outside of work, they access each other's humanity. This kind of experience occurs most frequently at organizations with highly engaged teams, though it isn't generally common. Less than half (45 percent) of employed Americans report feeling connected with others at work.

It will come as no surprise that the acceleration of hybrid and fully remote work arrangements in recent years has reduced the opportunity for these kinds of relationships to form organically, as so many workers spend fewer hours each month in the same physical space as their co-workers. In a global survey of 31,000 workers in thirty countries, Microsoft found that 43 percent of remote workers do not feel included in meetings, and only 27 percent of leaders say their company has developed hybrid meeting protocols to ensure everyone is included and engaged. The study also found that only half

---

* *No More Team Drama: Ending the Gossip, Cliques, & Other Crap That Damage Workplace Teams.* Available online, if you're interested.

of remote workers say they have a thriving relationship with their direct team, and even fewer (42 percent) report having a strong relationship with co-workers outside of their direct team. These experiences are a recipe for a continual exodus of talent from hybrid or remote roles, given the importance of belonging.

If you lead a hybrid or fully remote team, it's imperative to innovate in these aspects of belonging. This is not about navigating the individual preferences that workers often have about working on-site versus working from home.* Rather, leaders will need to find new and creative ways to cultivate virtual interactions that go beyond just work while simultaneously balancing the need to do so against, for lack of a better term, "Zoom fatigue." Among the questions I am asked the most at workshops and conferences is how to build connection among fully remote teams, or in organizations where some employees work on-site together and others do not. My answer is simple: we must get people laughing together and learning about each other beyond work topics.

There are ways to do this virtually. Many teams have taken to playing games and holding virtual contests as part of virtual meetings. Some companies hire virtual MCs and games masters to design and facilitate these kinds of experiences. There are even online Zoom games and third-party apps that can integrate with video conferencing platforms to bring these kinds of interactions to life. In addition to play and fun, taking a few minutes at meetings to learn more about colleagues can go a long way. Some virtual teams have members give home office tours, introduce their pet, or bring a favorite trinket to the meeting, all to help digital colleagues access each other's humanness more successfully.

---

* Many of these are born out of naturally occurring preferences for introversion and extraversion.

This is why every week on my *Boss Better Now* podcast we give listeners a Camaraderie Question of the Week. These are questions leaders can take to teams to help members form tighter connections and build camaraderie. (A list of some of these questions is included in the digital toolkit for this book found at employaltybook.com.) Beyond this kind of "mandatory fun," teams are also intentionally assigning virtual co-workers to collaborate more on various tasks and projects, even just in pairs, because the interactions that result from the work have the potential to boost familiarity and relationships.

Beyond these virtual tactics, the number one recommendation I make for helping virtual teams form better connections is to try and gather in person at least twice a year. Planning a team retreat once every six months seems to be the minimum frequency needed to form bonds out of the shared experiences that take place in person. The key is to make sure that these gatherings are not all work. You'll want to mix some business with social or teambuilding experiences that, as noted above, get people laughing together and interacting around things that have little to do with work. These twice-yearly gatherings can be built upon over time, provided there are also efforts taking place virtually in between them, to foster connection.

A case can be made for engaging in any of these kinds of activities for traditional in-person work as well, as they produce the same result: people interacting and learning about each other in ways that enhance connection.

Highlighting Contributions

The third element of belonging is contribution. When the individual talents, ideas, and efforts of team members are known to a team, there is understanding across the group of how that person is helping the team succeed. This adds significantly to belonging. This is yet another reinforcement of everything discussed about purpose in Chapter 8. When co-workers see and hear the personal ways their peers are contributing to their collective goals and success, it can drive unity. It also becomes a way to overcome differences in beliefs or identity that drive personal wedges between professional colleagues. As Deloitte's researchers wrote regarding contributions:

> Belonging based on contribution does not require people to agree on (for instance) their political views or conform to a single cultural template. Instead, it celebrates individuals' and teams' diversity of thought in ways that promote their commitment to shared outcomes, enabling them to engage in discussions that consider a variety of perspectives with the aim of coming to an agreement. When teams are united by a common purpose, differences in opinion on matters unrelated to that purpose can become less relevant—and differences in opinion on how to achieve that purpose become grounds for reasonable dialogue rather than a source of divisiveness.

To nurture this aspect of belonging, it's important for leaders to shine a light on the many ways individuals add to the performance and success of a team. Whether it be at meetings, in ongoing communication, or in casual conversation, a leader's willingness to highlight the ways in which people are contributing can drive belonging, even when the individual being discussed isn't in the room.

Be careful, though, to spotlight more than just accomplishments. Here, time and traits matter. Acknowledging the person on the team with the knack for keeping all the project data organized or the Administrative Assistant who did hours of unseen computer work is just as important to celebrate as winning an account. Without these intentional disclosures, the team might never get to fully understand or appreciate someone's contributions. These are the micro-experiences that leaders, and team members, must repeatedly create.

What's clear is that employees are abandoning noxious cultures of competition, exclusion, gossip, infighting, and tribalism. As Dr. Shirley Davis told me, belonging "is not HR's role or diversity's role, but every leader's responsibility. It is a global business imperative, if you want to attract top talent and have an organization that will not only thrive but be around for decades to come." Belonging rarely just happens. It must be attended to regularly, like most of the experiences at work that bring Employalty to life and activate commitment.

And the presence of belonging—and most of the other dimensions you've read about thus far in this book—is almost always determined by the single most influential factor in the employee experience: the boss.

Great Boss
Coaching
Trust
Advocacy

GREAT
BOSS

11

Coaching

I'VE NEVER "gone viral," but a few years ago, I came close. I was a few years into running my business teaching leaders how to be better bosses. It became clear to me around that time that I should be creating and sharing content via video. Short "how-to" videos, excerpts from workshops, clips from keynotes at conferences, and silly or inspiring vlogs* that support bosses at all levels were planned for the channel. I admit, I resisted the idea for a while. I was already writing a blog, publishing an email newsletter, and doing client work with organizations all over the country. My plate was full. I eventually dove in all at once because (insert facepalm emoji here) I'm someone who makes a living speaking and teaching, so video of me speaking and teaching is probably important in the era of smartphones and social media.

---

* Vlog is short for "video blog." This is a strange word to say, and even to read. It sounds more like the name of a Russian heavy in a Bond film than a term for a kind of online content, but now you know.

And so, my *BossBetter with Joe Mull* YouTube channel was born.*

At first, most of the videos we shared were geared toward leaders working in the healthcare profession, as we did most of our work in that industry for a time. Eventually, we broadened our content and our audience to leaders at all levels in all industries. We've shared nearly three hundred videos since we started. While none has gone viral, there is one video that has dramatically outperformed all others. It was released shortly after we started publishing vlogs. It has a hundred times more views than any other video we've shared. The title? "How Bosses Demoralize Employees."

This video isn't all that different from the other vlogs I've recorded and posted. It's me speaking directly to the camera, sharing tactics to overcome specific challenges related to managing people in the workplace.† The one thing that is different about this video, however, is that this time around, I focused on some problematic behaviors of bosses, not employees. In just over four minutes, I quickly catalogued more than a dozen habits some bosses have that negatively impact the morale of team members at work (and why they're so harmful). At the end, I invited viewers to comment. Specifically, I said this:

> Now it's your turn. What other ways do bosses demoralize teams? What have you experienced as an employee? What happens too often that does harm and limits success? Share your thoughts in the comments box below...

---

*   youtube.com/@bossbetter if you want to check it out. #ShamelessPlug
†   youtu.be/67YztHgt3Fw or just search the title. Oh, and this was a particularly bad hair day. Thanks for understanding.

And *wow*, did they ever. What followed was a deluge of stories and examples of bad boss behavior. To date, this video has received thousands of comments. Even at time of writing, five years after it was released, we still average one new comment every day from someone sharing their story. Many who comment simply want to acknowledge their agreement with the ideas I shared. The video is littered with comments like these:

My boss does everything you say in this video.

This dude must have worked at my company.

This video should be required viewing for every retail establishment.

Some had harsh words for bosses in general, while others were quite funny.

Narc bosses are straight from hell.

Would it be rude if I sent this video to my ex-boss?

We must have the same boss lady. Are you my co-worker? Mike? Amy? Is that you? Hah, jk, but seriously.

One person even wrote a scene.

Boss: Here is this task. It should take you 2 hours to do it.

Employee: Okay, sir.

**After one hour, boss shows up.

Boss: So are we done? We should have sent this to the customer already!

Employee: No sir, I need some more time.

**Boss sighs, demonstrating that he is upset.

Boss: It should have been done in two hours but go ahead.

Employee's morale, self-belief, and confidence shattered and continues.

But mostly, viewers used the comments section to vent. Underneath the video, they shared stories about their experiences with their bosses. Many are short, but detailed. Others are paragraphs long. Some are heartbreaking.

> I always treated others with respect, my attendance was great, and I always tried my best. But this manager wore me down from keen employee to I don't give a crap anymore... It's not worth it.

> I was attacked by a co-worker who is the boss's favorite (why do bosses always pick the lazy ones to be their favorites?). Nothing was ever fixed about the situation.

> There's so much negativity and stress at work. Our boss refuses to think it's her and not us. She made us all go to this meeting regarding "teamwork" but we all had no problems with each other. It's her.

> I just need a 5 min break on a shift. Please.

We can learn a lot about leadership from employees semi-anonymously commenting on their boss's behaviors on the internet. In a way, these thousands of comments became a fascinating kind of micro-lab to observe what employees really think of their bosses, how their leaders show up at work, and the types of habits and behaviors that do the most harm. Among the most prevalent kinds of comments were employees sharing examples of bosses acting in contradictory or hypocritical ways.

> I hate how we all get told not to text or call our boss if it's their day off, but on our days off that doesn't stop them and they get angry if we don't respond. We get yelled at for having so much to do and all of us are working as hard as we can, but our own boss doesn't even know how to register

patients so how can we ask her to help out when she herself doesn't know the job she is looking over?

Today my boss pulled me in his office and said I shouldn't have done a task he told me to do. The job was ended earlier than expected but he blamed me for getting too far ahead.

One of my pet peeves is being told to never have your cell phones out... and having a supervisor or the entire management staff openly using their phones and even flaunting the fact they are somehow above their own rules!

Three of us were very productive self-starters, working in high gear all the time. One was a slacker. He took long walks, took naps, shot the bull with people in other departments, spent hours managing a football poll, cheated on his timecard, took off Mondays for hangovers, and quit early on Fridays to go to a beer joint... my boss's solution was to promote him as team leader.

Employees don't just notice the obvious failings of their supervisors. They notice everyday interactions too.

Headquarters sent me a deadline I must complete today. My boss is mad I didn't take part in the Easter egg hunt or drive him to get lunch for the staff. These are grownups.

I just quit my job solely because the boss was full of gossip and [had a] bad attitude. If you're talking trash about your employees to me, I bet you're talking trash about me to your other employees.

The mind games, the making you feel like you should be lucky to have this job, the change your ideas just a little to call them his, the having to justify to him why you deserve your bonus when you outshine everyone. It blows me away that people like that can keep a business going. Let alone sleep at night.

Among these revelations and ruminations, you will occasionally find a comment from an empathetic employee who views their boss in a positive light, but needs more from them:

My former boss always struck me as a fair and decent woman but one thing that created tension was her habit of not indicating clearly to a person she saw as a troublemaker. Instead, she would use general warnings or say "some people" to us all. I feel it would be wiser if she spoke directly to a person... rather than continually warning all employees.

My current boss is wearing too many hats and needs an assistant. She won't get one, even though our company can afford to. I love her to death, and she can be so awesome, but she cannot retain and hire good staff for our retail floor. She's the only one with hire/fire power and I work with some STR8 up IDIOTS. She does not like to be the bad guy, but you know, someone has to be...

What we've long known through research—and what is painfully obvious after spending just a little bit of time reading comments like these—is that how bosses treat employees matters to employee commitment more than anything else you've read about thus far in this book.

The Boss Matters Most

There's a ubiquitous statistic that has been steadily making the rounds in books, in lectures, and on social media for years. I even used it in the YouTube clip referenced above. It's this one: 75 percent of people who quit a job say their boss is part or all of the reason why.

This finding can be traced back to research done by James K. Harter, PhD, and the Gallup organization, which studies employee engagement extensively. While there is some debate as to the exact statistical influence that bosses have on turnover—a more recent pre-pandemic study from Development Dimensions International (DDI) put the number at 57 percent—what's not in doubt is the enormous effect bosses have on each individual employee's experience. How bosses treat the people they supervise is the single biggest influence on employee commitment. If an individual contributor is able to work to their fullest potential, it's because their boss has engineered the environment that makes it possible. In one survey of 14,500 US workers, employees reported working to their full potential when six criteria are present:

1 They are clear about what they are expected to do.

2 They are willing to ask questions and feel safe doing so.

3 They are not overwhelmed with rules about how the work has to be done or with unproductive meetings.

4 Their organization supports creative problem-solving and provides rewards and recognition for jobs well done.

5 Their supervisors notice and acknowledge employee feelings, understand how their decisions will impact employees, and help them manage their emotions.

6 They see purpose and meaning in their work and are committed to their organization.

Look at that list and ask yourself this question: Where do each of these conditions come from? If I am an employee at your company, and I'm experiencing each of these criteria in my job, who is responsible for making that possible?

The answer, of course, is *my boss*.

If my expectations at work are clear, it's because of the communication and support I receive from my boss. If I feel safe asking questions or making mistakes, it's because my boss has created psychological safety. If I enjoy freedom on how to complete my work, can try creative problem-solving, and get rewards and recognition, these are all made possible by my boss. And on and on the list goes. In other words, if a team is performing at a high level, the leader is the primary reason why. Likewise, when a team is underperforming, the direct supervisor of those involved is likely the biggest culprit. That person is failing to meet the complex professional, emotional, and psychological needs of the members of that team. They aren't creating the conditions outlined above, which allow people to reach their fullest potential.

The outsized influence that bosses have on the employee experience has only increased since Covid-19 created so much workplace disruption. Post-pandemic research by McKinsey found that the top two reasons workers cited for leaving their jobs were that they didn't feel valued by their organizations (54 percent) or their managers (52 percent). We know this to be true: commitment comes from better bosses. If the employees in your organization are to experience Employalty, their direct supervisor is the primary delivery system.

But despite knowing for some time how important bosses are, it turns out we are stunningly incompetent at selecting and training those we name to the role.

We're Hiring the Wrong Bosses

A steady drip of research over the years has revealed that companies of all shapes and sizes consistently get this decision wrong. According to one study, only one in ten people possesses the necessary traits that great managers exhibit upon hiring. This is a tale as old as time.* Due to growth or a departure, the company needs to hire a new person to step into the role of leader. They look around at the available talent internally, invite applicants for the position publicly, and set about the task of evaluating interested candidates for the role. During the interview process, a candidate's years of experience, technical expertise, and success in a prior role are highlighted by the candidate and valued by selectors. The person who "interviews well" and checks all these boxes is then seen as qualified to lead. They are offered the position and they get to work. It doesn't take long for the new leader to discover that the problems they must navigate each day aren't related to their years of experience, technical expertise, or success in a prior role.

They're people management problems.

The questions new and inexperienced managers face each day are many. How do I motivate my team? How do I manage conflict between team members? How do I coach an underperforming employee? How do I navigate competing priorities between project groups? How do I respond to infighting or gossip on a team? How do I help a bored high performer evolve in their role? How do I unite the people who work here around a common purpose so they become more selflessly collaborative?

Too often those doing the hiring believe that if someone was great in a job, they'll be good at leading others who do

---

* If you started singing "Beauty and the Beast" here, you are my people.

that job. Again and again, this proves to be untrue. When it comes to choosing who to name manager, selectors consistently overvalue experience, technical expertise, and performance in a prior role. Simultaneously, attributes like warmth, patience, curiosity, and vulnerability are dramatically undervalued. It's also quite difficult to screen for less quantifiable skills like strategic thinking, empathy, and adapting one's style to work successfully with others whose style is dissimilar. These attributes, however, are among those most critical to the success of any leader who manages people.

As a result of this consistent prioritization of the wrong criteria, 60 percent of new leaders promoted or hired within our current era fail within two years. This is true at all levels of leadership: front-line, mid-level, and executive. In total, companies fail to choose the right talent for management positions 82 percent of the time. This is data compiled by Gallup from thousands of companies worldwide.

Think about how stunning that data is. Imagine you are considering six candidates for a leadership position. If you hung the pictures of your candidates on a dartboard and threw a dart blindfolded, the person chosen by the dart has a better chance of being the right person for the job than the person identified by your hiring committee.

So, who should we be hiring to lead teams?

The answer isn't a who, it's a what. As in *what* are the attributes of those who are most successful at leading teams? Decades of research in engagement, organizational development, and motivation, combined with my experience training leaders for more than fifteen years, point to three: coaching, trust, and advocacy. Great Bosses grant trust and work to earn trust from those they lead. Great Bosses consistently advocate for what is in the best interests of their direct reports. And Great Bosses actively deploy a skill that the

The belief that if
someone was great in
a job, they'll be
good at leading others
who do that job has
proven again and again
to be untrue.

———————

CEO of Gallup—an organization that has studied employee engagement across the globe for years—called the "silver bullet" of management. That skill is coaching.

A Great Boss Is a Coach

Forget the image that springs to mind when you hear the word "coach." For many of us, we picture the person in charge of our favorite sports teams. If you're imagining someone with a whistle and a visor who is barking out directions and correcting mistakes, that's not the kind of coach we're talking about. Coaching is the act of helping someone sort through what they know, think, and feel to determine their next actions.* A good coach listens intently, asks questions, and leaves the responsibility for determining next steps to the other person in the conversation. True coaching involves very little feedback or advice. The bulk of coaching is asking questions.

Here's an example. Imagine that one of your employees pops into your office waving some papers and says, "Hey, how did you want us to handle these requests for installations that came in past the deadline?" This is a topic you reviewed recently at a meeting. In the interest of speed, some leaders might just give the answer. Or perhaps you're tempted to reply with, "We just talked about that at the Ops meeting on Monday, don't you remember?" In a situation like this, coaching is an opportunity to assist the employee while also nurturing commitment. A coaching response might unfold like this:

---

* And taking no action is always an option too.

"Thanks for asking, Jim. What options do you see?"

[Jim pauses to think ...] "Well, the crews are fully booked already, so we can't guarantee the installs."

"Good point. But what can we do for them?"

"Well, if the schedule changes we might be able to fit them in. We should ... oh, that's right. We said we were going to run a wait list, right?"

"That's right. What's your next step?"

"I remember now. I'll let them know that they're on a wait list and that we'll get to them if room frees up on the schedule. I'll send an email."

"Is there a better way?"

"Than email? [Pause] I suppose a phone call is better, so they don't feel dismissed. [Laughing] Plus, I can answer all their questions at once instead of exchanging seven more emails."

"I love that you're thinking about how they'll take the news. Great job."

Notice in the example above that the boss almost exclusively asked questions. Plus how he asked those questions matters. He wasn't playing "gotcha" or sarcastically testing the employee. With coaching, you are patiently engaging in a supportive conversation designed to activate the employee's thinking. You help Jim sort through what he knows or thinks is the best path forward. You also praise his thinking and reinforce his instincts. In a conversation that likely took just sixty seconds, you made Jim feel knowledgeable, capable, and valued.

Coaching is an ideal response when someone has a question, or a problem, and we believe they have the information or insight to arrive at an answer.* A coach asks the right questions in the right order to create self-actualization. The conversation is driven by treating the person being coached as an expert and using questions to help that person sort through their expertise: What do you think? What do you know? What informs that thinking? How are you feeling about that? What do you want to accomplish? What does your gut tell you? What will happen if you go in that direction? What else could you try? What would you do if no one was here and you had to act alone? Amid these questions, a good coach acknowledges worthwhile ideas and insights while encouraging an examination of those that could be less effective or inaccurate. As a result, coaching conversations boost confidence, enhance creativity, spur critical thinking, create accountability, and prompt problem-solving.

Coaching also cuts down on the boss-has-all-the-answers routines many leaders fall into. Let me say that again: when the boss embraces their role as a coach, they don't have to have all the answers. With coaching, subject matter expertise is not required to guide anyone through an exploratory conversation. Conceptually, if an astronaut walked into my office tomorrow and was struggling with a problem on the International Space Station, I could coach that person. It doesn't matter that I'm the least astronauty person around,† because our interaction is not about me having answers. It's about

---

* Coaching is not appropriate when someone lacks the information or expertise needed, like a new hire for example. It's also not appropriate in urgent or crisis situations when direction and decisiveness are required.

† Seriously, I don't even like going up in *elevators*.

guiding the astronaut through a series of questions that helps her sort through her options and choose the best course of action, as determined by her.

This approach can be tricky for leaders. Some bosses are very good at telling others what to do. Many managers are in their role because they possess knowledge, they genuinely want to help, and they excel at directing. Others have come to derive their own value from the dependency others have on their knowledge and presence. Plus, coaching conversations can be slow and cumbersome at times. But a full-time command-and-control leadership style fails to deliver the psychological building blocks that lead to commitment. When employees are constantly directed, they don't experience critical thinking, autonomy, and ownership. Expecting employees to just *do* and not *think* robs them of their agency, which can spark boredom, resentment, and complacency. One thing that's become clear in all the job upgrading of the last decade is that employees *want* to be coached. They want to take an active role in learning and problem-solving. They want to partner with you in their development. They want mentorship.

Showing up as a coach, it should be noted, isn't just about the conversations leaders have. It's about the mindset we bring to our work with people in general. At the heart of coaching is setting aside judgment in favor of curiosity. Coaches operate with the assumption that people are both decent and capable. So when something goes awry, the leader seeks first to understand, not jump to conclusions.

For example, if you have an employee who starts consistently showing up late for work, resist the urge to decide that this person has stopped caring, can't manage their time, or is being careless. Instead, be curious. Ask yourself: What's happening here? What might be going on with this person that would cause them to show up in this way? What do they need that they're not getting? Then make time to hold this very conversation with the employee while refraining from judgment. "Hey, I noticed you've been late a few times in a row now. Are you okay? Help me understand what's happening..."

Coaching is *the* transcendent leadership skill. Show me a manager who has received training on how to be a coach *and* actively applied that training to their interactions with others, and I'll show you a leader with higher levels of commitment and retention on their team compared to others. These are the results that show up again and again in organizations that develop coaching leaders. Gallup's research has found that one meaningful coaching conversation each week can have a profound impact on engagement and retention. Likewise, the Workplace Wellness Trends survey found that organizations that engage in coaching for their employees have 65 percent less turnover.

When leaders coach, they create pathways to deliver many of the experiences this very book argues are key ingredients to creating a destination workplace. Coaching draws out employees' strengths, gives them purpose, accelerates belonging, develops trust, and sees you functioning as an advocate. In fact, if you can only make time to develop one skill among the leaders in your organization, an argument can be made that it should be this one.

Employalty is about creating a more humane employee experience. If you want people to commit to your organization, the people leading them must commit to showing up as a coach. This is the first dimension to operating as a Great Boss.

Next, leaders must grant and earn trust.

12

Trust

WHEN I ASK Dana Kelly about that job she accepted while sitting in the Burger King parking lot, her face lights up. "I hit the lottery," she says. "It's amazing. I wake up every day, and I can't wait to go to work."

Nearly two years after leaving her job at the excavation company, a job that obliterated her self-confidence and landed her in the hospital, she says it's her boss that has made all the difference. "When you're in a job where you're micromanaged to the point where you don't know the right answer anymore, you stop trusting yourself. I had to learn how to trust myself again, how to trust my instincts. My new boss was very helpful in that because he trusts me. Before, I was never allowed to do anything without it going under the nose of the manager. Now, I have the opportunity to make decisions and to be trusted."

Dana's new role has her heading up operations for a small management consulting firm. Almost from the beginning, her boss created an environment drastically different from the one she came from. It started with frequent check-ins on the scope of her duties. "He asks me, 'What do you want to do? What do you enjoy about your job? What are your goals?' He lets me grow and try new things." Her boss works collaboratively with her to tweak her role to align with her talents and interests. After nearly a decade of suffering an impossible-to-manage workload, Dana also finds the volume of her duties far more manageable at her new job. "I almost didn't know what to do with having time to breathe during my workday. To be able to have time to learn other things, or read up on something, or work more carefully on a project—my whole life is at peace."

Dana's enthusiasm for her work becomes obvious when she talks about what her employer does, which is design and deliver training solutions for small businesses. "Our clients are amazing people. We're really improving the lives of others. It gives you purpose, and you want to keep going because it's making a difference." She also loves her team ("There's so much mutual respect and compassion toward each other") and the flexibility her new position grants her. Dana has total freedom to set her own schedule, work from home at her discretion, and take time off whenever she wants. "That took some getting used to," she laughs. "There was no way I could take time off before, because the work would just pile up to a point of being unbearable. Now, I can have a life outside of work. I've been able to see my family that lives out of state. My life is completely and totally different now. I'm happier and healthier in a way I've never experienced before. My brother told me he wants to send my boss a message that says, 'Thanks for giving us our sister back.'"

By now you can probably see all the ingredients of Employalty reflected in Dana's story. She has a manageable workload, flexibility, purpose, work that aligns with her strengths, belonging, and a Great Boss. Though she took slightly less money to move into this role, she's getting nearly every other experience that leads to commitment, all while enjoying a much more humane employee experience. Remember Dana's Employalty Scorecard from Chapter 6? It now looks like this:

Dana Kelly's New Job Employalty Scorecard

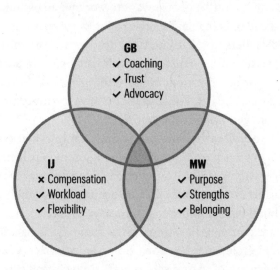

To hear Dana tell it, her newfound professional fulfillment and personal happiness all flow from the trust her new boss has granted her since she arrived. "My boss gives me the freedom to make mistakes. I get asked my opinion. My creativity and my ideas are embraced and encouraged. I feel smart again. It's such a silly thing, but it's changed my own self-worth."

To be a Great Boss, a leader must grant and earn trust. These are two distinct sets of behaviors, yet both are essential.

Earning Trust

David Horsager has been studying trust for most of his adult life. He's the author of the books *Trusted Leader* and *The Trust*

Edge, and his company produces an annual global study called the "Trust Outlook." According to the research he's spearheaded over three decades and across six continents, no other factor influences employee experience and company performance more than trust.* "The number one reason in first world countries that people want to work for an organization, even ahead of being paid more or a fun work environment, is trusted leadership. Without trust, leaders and organizations fail." David defines trust as a confident belief in a person, product, or organization. He says that a lack of trust is the biggest expense in an organization. "If you want to increase retention, you have to increase trust."

To be a leader who earns trust, David says, several patterns of behavior are required. Chief among them is pairing competence with humility. A perception of competence is critical to managers earning trust. Where teams perceive their leader as lacking certain knowledge or skills, problems arise. But there are certainly situations when someone is named to a leadership role, and they don't necessarily have competence in all the work of their direct reports. In nearly all situations a leader faces, but especially in these circumstances, leaders must be able to admit what they don't know. "Vulnerability goes a long way," David says. "One of our studies found that 92 percent of people would trust their senior leader more if they were more vulnerable about their mistakes." Where leaders lack competence, they must own it publicly, often, and with abject humility. Don't know how to do something? The worst thing you can do is pretend that you do.

Here the trait of knowing what you don't know is critical. The leader who doesn't understand but is unafraid to admit it

---

* It's possible that David has used the word "trust" more than any person alive... ever. If it was a world record, it would be his, hands down. He is that dialed in on the subject.

will be far more successful than the leader who fears looking incompetent. And that's the irony here, isn't it? Competence is so important that admitting I am incompetent in certain areas is itself an act of competence—in vulnerability, honesty, and avoiding perfectionism. It's a sacrificing of power and authority. You can't possibly know it all. When you don't, say so right away, and keep learning while elevating the voices of the experts around you.

Earning trust from the people we lead is also born out of doing the many things that are often synonymous with trust. "There are many touching synonyms for trust, like 'faith,' 'dependable,' 'reliable,' 'safety,' 'consistency'; there are other words we use," David says. "It's all trust." Engaging in these kinds of behaviors is how leaders build trust over time. While trust takes time to earn, David told me that it can be built quickly. "One way that trust gets built quickly is in crisis, because that usually amplifies who we really are in many ways. Another way is through what we call transfer trust. If Person A trusts Person B, and Person C trusts Person A but doesn't know Person B, and A says that B is trustworthy, that amplifies deeper trust." This trust transfer alone makes the case for every leader to work to build trusting relation- ships with as many individuals as possible in an organization, because those people that the leader engages with will ulti- mately spread more trust in that leader among those he or she interacts with that the leader doesn't often meet.

Trust is also rooted in people believing what you say. For this reason, leaders and business owners must follow through on their plans and keep their promises. We must also be transparent whenever possible. Among the biggest complaints from employees in organizations is that there is not enough communication from leadership. One study found that only 40 percent of employees feel well informed about their company's goals, strategies, and tactics. Yet this criticism shows up even in organizations who are committed to information-sharing and do it well. It's a kind of generic, expected, never-ending grievance.

For some, this complaint is rooted in what amounts to a normal and visible difference in access. As a leader, your employees know you are privy to information they don't have. They know you go to meetings and get updates about things outside their purview. The most trusted leaders share as much information as possible, as early as possible, and often without being prompted to do so. At times when you might not be permitted to disclose certain pieces of information, a trusted leader acknowledges the truth. They say, "there are some things going on behind the scenes that I'm not permitted to talk about yet, but I promise that I will share them with you as soon as I can." Then they immediately allay any fears or rumors that could potentially grow out of the mystery of not knowing. When leaders know more than they can say, covering up that they have knowledge or omitting it altogether can damage trust, whereas the tacit acknowledgment above goes a long way to earning trust.

Another common way that leaders earn trust is by working alongside their employees whenever possible. The restaurant manager who buses tables, helps cook during the dinner rush, or packages takeout orders can't be accused by employees of not understanding what they go through on a regular basis. Navigating the same challenges employees face by working with them is a tangible way to seed the belief, among employees, that "my boss understands what we deal with." Pitching in with your team from time to time also anchors your understanding of what employees face in real-world experience rather than just second-hand information.

While leaders must work to earn trust over time and not assume that it will be granted freely from employees, they must simultaneously operate in reverse with employees. To nurture commitment, leaders must grant trust to employees often before it is earned.

Granting Trust

Sixteen months into the Covid pandemic, I delivered the opening keynote at a conference for a national network of cancer centers. I discussed many of the core ideas in this book, about what organizations must do to become a destination workplace amid a competitive job market. As you can imagine, there was an emphasis on flexibility, and I spent time discussing the surge in remote work brought about by the pandemic. Afterwards, I found myself chatting with a hospital administrator in the convention center lobby. "The problem with remote," he said, "is you can't see the employees. You don't know what they're doing, if they're working, if they're double-dipping and taking extra jobs on the side... I just don't know how to make it work."

"Well," I replied, "those problems you just listed have nothing to do with remote work. Those are problems of trust."

For many leaders there is a fundamental assumption that, left to their own devices, employees will lie, cheat, game the system, do the minimum, and rip off the company. We can see these beliefs manifested in the complex systems employers install to monitor work or in the cumbersome processes they require for employees to constantly check in or report work. Recent news coverage of such efforts around remote work has been startling, with some companies counting keystrokes, monitoring attendance with cameras, and even requiring hourly updates. These systems that companies enact to monitor and track work are almost always driven by fear of the rare bad apple. They are there, many leaders say, to blunt the temptation of loafing or to catch those who would cheat or steal. The problem is that we then impose these systems on a workforce largely composed of ethical people. The result is a set of systems that send a powerful message from management to employees over and over again: "We don't trust you."

The truth is, the overwhelming majority of people are trustworthy. Most employees working remotely aren't going to nap, watch Netflix, and ignore their work because suddenly no one is watching them. They're going to do the best they can, in part because they're grateful for the chance to work virtually and want to prove they can be just as effective. But also because most people are good people who take pride in their work. Gallup has been publishing research on remote workers for years (and long before Covid spiked the number of employees working virtually). They've consistently found that remote workers are three times as likely to be engaged at work as long as they get ongoing feedback from their boss.

Here again, the Myth of Lazy shows itself operating in the background. When leaders push, cajole, and monitor their employees, it is because they believe that people are generally inclined to do the minimum—that they are unreliable and inconsistent unless we stay on top of their every move. This doubt and cynicism erodes morale on teams, seeds a relationship of mistrust, and ultimately breeds self-preservation. But studies show that when we see people as trustworthy—as reliable and striving for more on our behalf without needing to be coaxed or pressured—we create an environment that cultivates commitment.

You can see that proof in Dana Kelly's story above and in the social science research on trust—and its importance in the workplace—that has emerged in recent years. In organizations where employees enjoy high amounts of trust from their leaders, workers report 74 percent less stress, 106 percent more energy at work, 50 percent higher productivity, 13 percent fewer sick days, 76 percent more engagement, 29 percent more satisfaction with their lives, and 40 percent less burnout. Trust has a major impact on employee loyalty as well. Compared with employees at low-trust companies, 50 percent more of those working at high-trust organizations planned to stay with their employer over the next year, and 88 percent more said they would recommend their company to family and friends as a place to work.

Employees who aren't trusted by their boss at work often use one word to describe that leader: micromanager. According to one study, 59 percent of employees said they've worked for a micromanager during their career. Micromanaging includes tracking employee movements, overmanaging steps, details, and decisions, and taking away independence. Micromanagers resist delegating, correct tiny details, take back work that is incomplete or in draft stages, and discourage decision-making without their approval. Employees who have worked under this style of leadership describe feeling as though they aren't permitted to think, only to do what they are told—exactly as they are told. These conditions rob people of their autonomy and prevent them from unleashing their creativity, two essential components of intrinsic motivation. When people are managed in this way, it hurts productivity, decreases morale, and accelerates quitting.

Where it gets tricky is that most leaders who are micromanagers don't see themselves that way. They'll say they are efficient or that they are standardizing processes in the name of quality.

What's truly happening is that they don't trust their team members.

Putting Trust to Work

Where trust is lacking, innovation can be stifled; where trust is given, innovation can flourish. Consider two sales professionals working at two different trade associations. Peter works for a boss who says, "We need to start recruiting sponsors for our big annual convention. Here are the sponsorship packages we'll offer. Here's the list of the companies you should target. Here are the scripts for what to say in your outreach calls or emails and a schedule for when to do them. Here's a chart that outlines how often we should follow up with prospects." At the same time, the other salesperson—let's call him William—has a boss who says, "I need you to start signing up sponsors for our annual convention. Take a look at who we've worked with historically and the packages we've offered, and make a plan for who we'll target and how we'll get them involved this year. If you're comfortable, you can start recruiting partners right away."

On the one hand, Peter's boss gave him a project along with detailed steps that the boss expected would be followed. For his association, they likely know roughly how many partners will sign up to be sponsors and the expected revenue they'll generate based on what they've done in previous years. Peter is executing this plan exactly as his boss instructed. William, on the other hand, wasn't given a detailed plan. His boss gave him responsibiity for a project and a few key instructions, then encouraged him to dive in and proceed as he saw fit. If William is skilled, he can take things from there. If he's unsure of how to operate at any step of the project, coaching and feedback from his boss will help him work it out. Both approaches can lead to satisfactory completion of the projects, but what's worth noting here is that only William has a chance of generating better-than-expected results for his company.*

In William's case, that's exactly what happened.

William is a colleague of mine. When he was charged with selling event sponsorships but not given a predetermined set of steps to adhere to in the process, he ended up driving a whole new level of success for his organization's annual conference. William created a target list from sources his boss would have never considered. He developed innovative packages that looked quite different from what the organization had previously offered sponsors. He more frequently and directly solicited prospects than any salesperson had done in prior years. The result was that William generated more than twice the sponsorship revenue and three times as many partners for their event than his association ever had before.

By giving William more autonomy and the creative freedom to execute, his boss made these results possible. For Peter, they were never in the cards. William also enjoyed his work far more than Peter would have. In the example above, Peter doesn't get to be creative. Peter doesn't get to engage in trial and error. Peter doesn't get to try out his ideas and then reap the psychological rewards that come when they work. Peter is simply there to follow a checklist. Don't think, Peter. Just do.

"The easiest way to increase trust, especially in a virtual world, is to align on outcomes," David Horsager says. "It's not about how they spend their time or if they worked between eight and five. Maybe they did, or maybe they worked a little bit more at night, or they did the whole thing in five hours because they're so capable—that doesn't matter. Care about

---

* Knowledge and experience matter here. If William was new or untrained, he might need more support from his boss. Granting too much trust to someone who doesn't know how to proceed can be frustrating and scary.

Employees who enjoy
high amounts
of trust from leaders
report less stress,
more energy, higher
productivity, and less
burnout.

_____

the outcomes. We increase trust by aligning on outcomes because it creates both freedom and accountability." In William's case, that's exactly what his boss did.

Granting trust to employees means that leaders must find ways to let employees execute on their work product in their own ways. It means we're willing to let them go through trial and error, which we know is an integral part of learning. Operating in this way can be hard for leaders and business owners, as it requires that you allow people to fail from time to time. In a business world competing for every dollar and customer, that can be a tough pill for some to swallow. While failure that inflicts lasting damage on a team or organization should be minimized wherever possible, mistake-making and the learning it produces is an expected and important part of the journey of granting trust. Where employees are appropriately trained, allow them, as much as possible, to manage people and execute projects in their own way. This is what employees want. A Citigroup and LinkedIn survey found that nearly half of employees would give up a 20 percent raise for greater control over how they work.

We've met a few bosses in this book whose way of operating earned the trust of their employees. Jack Merrill gave his HVAC team in Kentucky a substantial amount of autonomy to manage their work and schedules independently. Dana Kelly's new boss mined her for ideas almost as soon as she arrived and then gave her broad oversight of her work product. So, too, did Paige McMullen's new boss at the long-term care facility. Sean Goode at Choose 180 asked for a higher standard of professionalism from his team and then trusted them to deliver, which they have. These are leaders who consistently engage in the behaviors that grant employees trust. They don't assign tasks, they delegate responsibilities. They coach employees through mistakes, confusion, or substandard work. They empower their employees to make the best decisions they can without having to wait for or rely on their supervisor signing off. They constantly ask for opinions, ideas, and insight, and assign weight to what is offered. These are the actions that leaders must take to grant trust.

Of the three factors that create employee commitment, Great Boss is consistently the most vulnerable in an organization. While several aspects of the Employalty model can be institutionalized—like generous compensation or position flexibility—who we designate to lead and how they show up can create inconsistency in the employee experience. Just as commitment is fragile, so, too, is the perception of a leader as a Great Boss. This is in part because it takes years to earn trust and goodwill as a leader, yet it can all be nullified quickly in a flurry of bad choices or upsetting interactions. Go back to the previous chapter and look more closely at the comments left on that YouTube video I featured. Nearly all of the complaints that employees shared about their bosses—from gossip, to stealing credit, to failing to address toxic people—are about behaviors that sabotaged trust. "I've seen it happen," David Horsager told me. "Years of trust can be lost in a moment."

Yet when trust is both granted and earned, it creates transformation. It nurtures commitment. Dana Kelly is proof. "In my old job, there was nothing that was just mine, nothing that I had ownership over that I was just trusted with. It really does affect your day-to-day work. It almost makes you feel demeaned. If your employees aren't offered that opportunity, they'll feel stunted. Now my boss trusts me. I have important work that lives with me that he trusts me and relies on me to do well. That's inspiring. It's a totally different feeling. When I get asked my opinion, it makes me feel so valued, even if the opinion isn't used. Having a boss who trusts me... it breathes life into working."

If you are the new leader of a team, or you onboard a new hire, know that each person starts their relationship with you with differing levels of trust. Because people come to our workplaces with a variety of prior experiences, some employees will trust you early, until you give them reason not to. Others will doubt you first until you prove that you can be trusted. And some people may never fully trust you, solely because you hold the title of leader. To earn commitment, you will have to earn trust slowly while granting it quickly.

As David Horsager told me, "Everything of value is built on trust. Trust is always the leading indicator of success and the root cause of problems. The only reason you follow a leader is trust." Start with the belief that your employees have integrity. Treat them as humans with scruples and employees with talents. Then define goals, discuss progress periodically, give feedback, and provide support. That's the trust recipe.

Beyond granting and earning trust, a Great Boss cares about his or her people beyond the tasks and duties of their job. He or she also prioritizes their humanity, champions their professional path, campaigns for resources, and defends them against those who could do harm or derail professional success. This is a set of behaviors that consistently leads employees to join, stay, care, and try. It's a set of behaviors I've come to refer to with a single word: advocacy.

13

Advocacy

JEREMY EASTON knew he was having a heart attack.

As he got the restaurant kitchen opened for the day, the chest pains he had experienced off and on over the weekend were back. Between turning on the ovens, starting the steam tables, and hauling buckets of sanitized water to each cooking station, he started sweating abnormally. He'd spent the weekend pushing aside the idea that he might have something going on with his heart, but his prior training as an EMT now made his symptoms impossible to ignore.

He knew he should go to the hospital, but he hesitated.

Jeremy had only been working at the Italian restaurant for two months. He was hired to be second in command of the kitchen, with the expectation that he would replace the head chef soon. After thirty years of cooking in restaurants, Jeremy knew that his absence would be an issue. "When the leader in the kitchen disappears, that creates a problem," he told me. His mind raced. Should he ask the owner, who had entered the building a few minutes after him, for permission to go to the emergency room? Would his new employer think he was just trying to get out of work? Was he overreacting? With symptoms too distressing to ignore, Jeremy decided to approach his boss.

"Hey, I'm having some chest pains. I'm gonna go get checked out."

The owner's eyes widened. "Do... do you want me to drive you to the hospital?" Jeremy declined. "If they tell me I'm fine, I'll be back. If I'm not... well... we'll see what's going on." Jeremy drove himself fifteen minutes to the emergency room where the medical team there confirmed that, yes, he was actively experiencing a heart attack. After a flurry of activity to get him stabilized, Jeremy tried to tell the ER doctor that he needed to get back to work. The doctor scoffed.

"You are in the midst of a heart attack. If you leave, it will be against medical recommendation, and you will likely die."

Jeremy had no choice but to stay. He was prepped quickly for surgery, and in the hours that followed had an emergency stent put in and a blood clot removed from behind his heart. A second surgery followed days later, where additional stents were put in place. Though his heart was damaged, his doctors say he dodged a bullet. At only forty-six years old, Jeremy will be on heart medication for the rest of his life. After a few days in the hospital, Jeremy convalesced at home before returning to his job at the restaurant. All told, he missed two weeks of work as a result of his cardiac event.

A few days after being back in the kitchen, his paycheck arrived for the period he was out. He glanced at the paystub, expecting a minuscule amount, given all the time he had missed. Instead, his deposit was for a full two weeks of pay.

"I was really surprised," Jeremy said. "The owner paid me for both of the weeks I missed work. That just doesn't happen in the restaurant industry. You don't work, you don't get paid. He didn't have to do that."

Paying him for his time away wasn't the only thing the restaurant owner did when Jeremy fell ill. Although Jeremy had only worked at the restaurant for eight weeks, the owner called the hospital every day that Jeremy was there. When Jeremy was alert, his boss called his cell phone to check on him. He constantly asked the patient if he needed anything, like money, company, or help at home. The owner also talked frequently with Jeremy's girlfriend, who lived a considerable distance away and was commuting back and forth during Jeremy's hospitalization. During each call, he offered help. He said he would get her a place to stay, rides if she needed them, and drop food off at the hospital any time if it would be helpful.

"He was very kind," his girlfriend says. "He was genuinely worried about Jeremy."

When he reflects on his boss's actions during his recovery, Jeremy comes back to being unexpectedly paid for the time that he missed. "This was early December, so that money pretty much secured Christmas for my kids," he says, pausing to swallow the emotion of the memory. "I never had a boss do anything like that." Months after his heart attack, Jeremy is grateful, and not just for his recovery. He's thankful for the humanity extended to him during such a difficult time from a boss who had only just begun to get to know him.

"When someone treats you well and genuinely cares about you like that, it just makes you want to work harder for them."

Person over Position

Advocacy, put simply, is acting in another person's best interests. That's what Jeremy's boss did when Jeremy had a heart attack. The restaurant owner was concerned first and foremost with Jeremy's well-being and consistently acted in ways that made that apparent. Did he face challenges created by Jeremy's absence? Of course. Was he worried about the customer and business impact of being down a lead chef for two weeks? Without question. But Jeremy's boss understood that Jeremy isn't just a cook. He's a father. He's someone's brother. He has a girlfriend. He's a whole person with a full life, only a small portion of which is defined by his labor or his employment. And so, in the middle of a personal crisis, Jeremy's boss prioritized *Jeremy* above his own business interests.

This is what Great Bosses do. They engage in ongoing advocacy for the person first, position second. In the short term, it certainly cost the restaurant owner money to pay Jeremy for his time away. In the long term, however, that cost is a drop in the bucket compared to the loyalty, effort, and commitment triggered by Jeremy's boss's generosity.

If having a Great Boss is a central ingredient to Employalty, then advocacy is a central ingredient to being a Great Boss. There are a number of ways that leaders at all levels of an organization engage in advocacy on behalf of their team members.

Advocacy is caring about the person over the position. In this way, Great Bosses rarely ask an employee to prioritize their job or work before their family or health. In places where employees are consistently expected to miss soccer games and dance recitals, date nights and family gatherings, or rest and downtime, commitment is low. People quit. They can only endure the subjugation of the rest of their life to their job for so long.

Advocacy also requires bosses to care about the employee's long-term career as much or even more than the time they spend in their current role or with their existing employer.

Great Bosses accept that an employee's time in a position may be limited if that job hinders their ability to earn more, do what they love, or experience better quality of life. I cannot tell you the number of employees I've met who have told me stories of being offered an exciting new role within their current company only to have their supervisor decline the transfer, saying, "I can't afford to lose her right now. Can we revisit this in six months?" As you've heard several times in this book, this obliterates commitment because it prioritizes company operations over an employee's life, career, and finances. When this happens, not only does the employee leave the role, they also almost always leave the company.

Ensuring that employees have the information, materials, and equipment they need to successfully do their jobs is another form of advocacy. Outdated computers, a lack of needed supplies, or lax communication all hamper an employee's effectiveness. Great Bosses do what it takes to give people what they need to thrive in their role. Relatedly, advocacy also includes protecting and defending teams. When decisions or actions are taken that could inflict suffering, a Great Boss pushes back, doing all that they can to minimize a negative impact on their people and teams.

Advocacy also requires leaders to absorb blame and distribute credit. When failure occurs on a team or project, a Great Boss says "this is my fault." When accomplishments are achieved, a Great Boss is quick to say "credit goes to … ," naming a person or team.

Jeremy's comment about his boss's generosity making him want to work harder isn't just anecdotal. When employees perceive compassion or kindness from their leaders, loyalty skyrockets. This applies to when employees make mistakes too. Compassion is a far more powerful motivator than angry correction. In other words, shouting, "What were you think-ing, you idiot?!" when someone makes a mistake only does harm to that person's commitment and aptitude. Asking "Are you okay?" and later saying calmly, "That was a big mistake that can never happen again, understand?" actually super-charges commitment and aptitude, because it avoids shaming the employee and instead treats them with respect.* Part of advocacy is showing up with compassion even in the face of frustration.

These habits that I've come to call advocacy are important because they are the gateway to how employees perceive their work experience. That perception, in turn, shapes the degree to which employees deploy discretionary effort in their jobs. Advocacy also determines the degree to which supervisors can activate and influence employee behavior and motivation. How? It comes down to whether that leader operates from the limited influence of positional authority or from the more powerful locus of relational authority.

Positional vs. Relational Authority

Positional authority is the power inherently granted to some-one in an organization by their title or position alone. When a leader is given a role that comes with delegated power over a group of people, they immediately possess positional author-ity. They can give directions. They can make decisions. They are a source of information. They can impose penalties or terminate employment. Positional authority isn't earned, it is bestowed—not by employees, but by the organization.

---

* See "Why Compassion Is a Better Managerial Tactic Than Toughness" in the *Harvard Business Review*.

Relational authority, conversely, is the influence someone earns as a result of having developed a relationship with someone. Where mutual admiration, trust, and respect are present, relational authority is nurtured and gives the leader the ability to influence behavior without having to resort to coercion.* Trust, as discussed at length in the previous chapter, contributes greatly to relational authority. So, too, does advocacy.

For example, think of the worst boss you ever had. Now imagine that he or she comes to you late on Thursday and asks, "Can you come in and work on Saturday?" How are you feeling? What narrative is playing out in your head? If you're like most people, you're doing a cost-benefit analysis. You likely don't want to work on what was supposed to be your day off, but you mentally evaluate what it will cost you to say no, or what you will get in exchange for saying yes. Your answer likely comes down to a simple calculus: *do I have to do this?*

Now think of the best boss you ever had. Imagine that he or she comes to you late on Thursday and asks, "Can you come in and work on Saturday?" How are you feeling? How are you weighing this decision in your mind? While your availability certainly factors in, you know your boss cares about your life outside of work and probably wouldn't ask unless he or she was in a bind. You may not want to say yes, but part of you feels a sense of obligation. Maybe you think to yourself, *My boss always has my back; this is my chance to have theirs.* In the moment, you make a choice to say yes. Therein lies the biggest difference between positional authority and relational authority: the latter leads employees to *want* or *choose* to act.

---

* Much of our understanding about these two ideas is rooted in the literature and research on Self-Determination Theory (SDT) published by Edward Deci and Richard Ryan.

Here's another example. Imagine you're sitting at a restaurant, heavily salting the meal the waiter just dropped off. Seeing this, the waiter says, "I'm worried about you. Maybe you should cut down on the salt." What are the chances his observation will lead to you reconsider your salt intake? Probably very little.* Now imagine that same scenario, but this time, instead of the waiter saying it to you, it was your son or daughter in the seat across from you. If you're dumping salt on your meal and your child says to you, "I'm worried about you. Maybe you should cut down on the salt," it likely gives you pause, certainly more so than if the waiter had said it. Here's someone who cares about you. They're acting in your best interests. At a minimum, you don't find their observation out of bounds. Quite possibly, it leads to you giving it consideration. The relationship you have with your child grants them some relational authority† that potentially influences your thinking or behavior.

Meet Their Needs

When positional authority is exercised, employees have to comply. With relational authority, employees often act by choice, in some circumstances even engaging in behavior or thinking they might have otherwise avoided. Take, for example, the story of Jim, an IT Developer who quit his job after his boss canceled his holiday vacation time. Jim's story appeared in the media after getting thousands of views and

---

* It's more likely that you'll think, *Gee, thanks for the unsolicited and intrusive advice about what I put in my body, total stranger.*

† In research and publications, relational authority has also been called "referent power," "personal authority," and "soft power."

comments on Reddit. "I save my vacation days to take off the week after Christmas. I spend it with my kids. This time is very precious to me." In his post, Jim explains that his request to take off the last week of December was submitted and approved by his boss back in July. As November turned to December, Jim kept asking for the information he needed to finish an end-of-year project for a client. Since the project was tied to government auditing, it was time sensitive and had to be completed by December 31. At the time, Jim was the only developer in the company with the skill set to complete this type of client work. For more than two weeks, Jim repeatedly asked for the materials. They never came. As the holidays approached, he asked again and again, even offering to work extra hours in the run-up to Christmas to ensure the project's completion. After nearly three weeks and just hours before his holiday break was scheduled to begin, his boss finally sent over the information. Jim asked, "Who should I walk through the project with because I'm off after Christmas?"

Jim's boss said, "I'm sorry, but I have to ask you to work. I declined your time off next week."

When Jim asked what would happen to his vacation time, his boss said the company rules dictate that any accrued time not used by the end of the year is forfeited. In addition to having his days off revoked, Jim was told that he would forfeit his earned vacation time. After weighing his options, Jim did what so many workers dream of doing when getting royally screwed by their boss.

He quit.

What happened next was a barrage of texts and phone calls from his boss that morphed from begging to attacking.

You made your point. You can have today off if you call me and let me know when we can expect you tomorrow...

I'm asking you as a friend and not a manager to reconsider and call me.

Just call me and we will figure out your vacation.

Quit being so full of yourself. Be a team player.

You should be a better businessperson and give us two weeks' notice.

Maybe you shouldn't have planned for time off in December.

Do you know what your actions are going to do to the company? Peoples' jobs are on the line.

Pick up, HR wants to conduct their exit interview.

Pick up your phone.

ANSWER YOUR PHONE!!!

Jim's boss threatened to tell everyone in the company that their bonuses and holidays were being ruined by Jim. At one point, he pulled the emergency contact info from Jim's employment file and began calling Jim's wife's and father's phone numbers.

It will come as no surprise to you, I'm sure, that Jim never returned to that company. Though we don't have a lot of insight into the kind of relationship Jim had with his boss, the circumstances above paint a picture of a supervisor who engaged in zero advocacy for Jim. As a result, Jim's boss had no relational authority. If he had, things may have played out differently. Perhaps Jim gets what he needs well in advance of his scheduled vacation. Perhaps Jim delays his departure to get the project started. At a minimum, perhaps Jim stays with the company. While we can't say for sure, I'm certain that had Jim's boss engaged in advocacy, Jim's story would have played out differently.

How could Jim's boss have been a better advocate? He could have driven more intentional planning and communication in regard to the December project. He could have amplified Jim's earlier requests for materials. He could have lined up internal or external help in the event the project materials weren't received until Jim was scheduled to be out. When the materials arrived late, he could've sat with Jim and asked, "Can we come up with a plan that gets this off the ground before you leave while still preserving most of your time off?" If any of these steps had been taken, it may have created an entirely different result for Jim, Jim's boss, and the company.

While we don't know that these things didn't happen, how Jim's boss communicated with Jim about his resignation leads me to believe that they did not. Notice what happened as the situation devolved. At first, the boss's solution was simply to cancel Jim's time off. As he saw it, the company's priorities were more important than Jim's. When Jim held fast to his priorities and resigned, the boss started trying to entice him to return by finding a way to attend to Jim's priorities. Early on these things weren't possible (days off, carrying forward vacation time), then suddenly they were! Jim was offered a single day back. Then he was offered to carry forward his vacation time. Only when the company experienced pain did they begrudgingly work to attend to Jim's priorities. But Jim had had enough.

When his employer's first reaction to his conscientiousness—trying to attend to the project for weeks before being away—was simply to cancel the time off he'd had planned for half a year, Jim experienced a deep values violation. It was one that would not be overcome by any amount of backpedaling, threats, or enticement by his boss thereafter. Yet, if Jim had experienced more advocacy from his boss over time and earlier in this situation, there's a greater likelihood that this story wouldn't have ended with the project incomplete and Jim's job vacant.

The seeds of Employalty are planted and cultivated in many ways, as outlined in this book, but perhaps none is more obvious or frequent than advocacy. Showing up as an advocate for employees doesn't require grand gestures or months of formal training. At its core, advocacy is about caring about people and making that explicit.

Want to get better at advocacy? Some questions for your consideration:

- Do you know all of your employees' names?*

- For the people you see regularly, do you know at least part of their story? Do they have kids? Are they married? Do they live nearby or have a long commute? Do you make small talk or find things in common with them that have little to do with work?

- Beyond attending to even a basic kind of familiarity with people, do you see your employees as having knowledge and expertise? Every single person working for you knows more about something than you do, just by the nature of the chair they sit in or the work they touch daily. Do you ask their opinions? Do you seek their feedback?

- Do you ask about their challenges or how changes impact them? Do you talk with them about their career long term? Have you asked about any goals they have in their current position, career overall, or life outside of work?

---

* Remarkably, I constantly meet leaders who tell me they don't need to know everyone's names. The belief that you don't need to know the names of the people who work daily in the same space as you do is the very essence of dehumanization.

Nearly nine out
of ten bosses believe
they are leading
well, yet fewer than two
out of ten employees
say that they are.

———————

Have you provided support that moves them closer to these goals?

- Have you spoken up on their behalf when they're not in the room to protect them from work suffering? Do you actively work to understand the supplies, info, support, or respect they need to be effective, then campaign for these things in your organization?

- When employees experience illness, emotions, or personal struggles, do you demonstrate caring? Do you extend compassion?

- When employees' job duties or schedule get in the way of personal obligations or opportunities that are important to them, do you work to find compromises?

These are the actions of advocacy that turn leaders into Great Bosses in the eyes of their workers. If you want to spark commitment and retain talented people, you must work to make these habits common among your managers. In fact, all three of the dimensions that make up the Great Boss factor—coaching, trust, and advocacy—have to be in place. To compete for talent, Great Bosses must become common in your organization, from the CEO all the way down to front-line managers.

A Great Boss Is Required

In 2016, McKinsey surveyed more than fifty thousand supervisors and asked them to rate themselves as leaders. Specifically, they were asked to rate the degree to which they were effective role models of the desired behaviors they wished to see from their employees. Of all respondents, 86 percent expressed confidence that they were consistently leading by example. That same year, a separate study asked over eighty thousand employees to rate their leader's ability to effectively manage them. Less than 18 percent felt their leader was effective.

This is a stunning disconnect. Nearly nine out of ten bosses believe they are leading well, yet fewer than two out of ten employees say that they are. This gap is everywhere. It's almost certainly present in your organization as you read this. And the path to closing that gap is via coaching, trust, and advocacy—the three dimensions of being a Great Boss.

None of the advice and strategies outlined in this book can be executed without Great Bosses. The compensation, workload, and flexibility that create an Ideal Job for employees is facilitated at the ground level by Great Bosses. If employees get to do Meaningful Work—work that gives them purpose and aligns with their strengths in an environment where they feel they belong—it's because their boss is actively facilitating such an experience. So you can't skip this one. And you can't do Great Boss in half-measures. Candidly, if you're only going to dial in on one section of this book, it should be this one. In fact, a more equitable and honest representation of our Employalty model—one that accurately represents the ratio of influence each area has on the employee experience—should probably look like this:

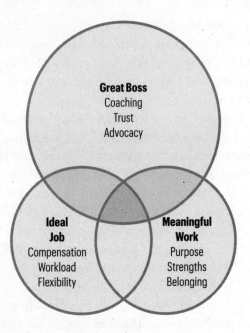

That's how influential a Great Boss is to Employalty. For some, you may have to completely recalibrate what you've long believed the job of a manager is. Do you believe that a boss's job is to manage to metrics, create schedules, drive productivity, acquire customers, enforce policies, and so on? Or do you believe that their job is to create the kind of employee experience that leads people to become committed? Yes, they can do both, but the latter must be the priority, and those other obligations must never be executed at the expense of the employee experience. Instead of managing schedules, tasks, and projects, the primary responsibility of bosses must be coaching, trust, and advocacy.

Now more than ever before, employees from all industries are rejecting unnecessary suffering at work. As such, they are rejecting, in all forms, the prospect of working for a bad boss.

If you want to have any hope of attracting talent, positioning them to become psychologically committed, and enticing them to stay, you must insist on better bosses.

Now that we've explored all the factors of Employalty at length, it's time to start the Employalty movement in your organization. If you're looking for guidance on how to assess where you are currently and get the ball rolling on the changes that will turn your organization into a destination workplace, simply read on. The next chapter provides a road map for putting all that you've learned into action.

14

Starting an Employalty Movement in Your Organization

THIS ENTIRE BOOK is built on a simple premise: outstanding results in business are most accessible by treating employees extremely well.

Is this a revelatory insight or just common sense? On the surface, it seems like the latter. But I know the truth. I've spent years studying commitment in the workplace. Despite decades of research in employee engagement, thousands of books written each year on leadership, and an infinite number of blogs and articles published on these topics every single day, it's clear: most leaders and business owners still don't understand the ingredients that lead to commitment and retaining employees.

But now you do.

The Employalty model you've just learned provides the simple framework leaders need to find and keep employees, unlock their commitment, and level up your company's performance. Giving employees their Ideal Job (via compensation, workload, and flexibility) doing Meaningful Work (from purpose, strengths, and belonging) for a Great Boss (via coaching, trust, and advocacy) is the blueprint to getting employees to join, stay, care, and try. It's how you turn your enterprise into a destination workplace. If you're ready to put this framework into action at your company, below are suggested steps and a collection of tools to help you get started.

Taking Action

As someone—probably a doctor—famously said, treatment without diagnosis is malpractice. That's why your first step should be to assess the current state of your organization against the Employalty Scorecard. Are your employees already experiencing any of the nine dimensions outlined in this book? There are ways to find out.

First, you can ask your team members. I've created a simple ten-question survey you can administer to your teams to get a snapshot of what's working well already and where you have deficits. You can download the Dimensions of Employalty survey, which is part of the free Employalty toolkit, over at employaltybook.com.

In place of or in addition to the survey, I strongly suggest that you open a dialogue with your workforce to better understand what is and is not working well across the three factors of Ideal Job, Meaningful Work, and Great Boss. You can do this via focus groups, interviews, or by adding open-ended questions to your survey that ask employees to tell you more. Many of the questions on the stay interview that's included in the toolkit (and that was mentioned in Chapter 9, on strengths) can be used for this purpose. As part of the assessment phase, you can even do a SWOT analysis on the Employalty framework; across the nine dimensions, where are your strengths, weaknesses, opportunities, and threats? Such an exercise should include leaders at all levels of the organization—who must be encouraged to speak freely and without fear of retaliation about their observations.

Once you've gathered insight, you'll next want to make a plan. I suggest creating three simultaneously: a 30-day, 90-day, and 180-day plan. Identify the actions you'll need to take to improve in the areas of greatest need that your assessment phase identified. The immediate 30-day plan should include any additional research or information gathering you need to conduct. For example, you may decide you need to do a market wage study for your industry or evaluate the various workloads of employees in the organization. Also, include in this 30-day plan any quick wins you can create right away for employees. Fill the later plans with the meetings, training, and project groups you'll need to begin implementing or improving in the nine dimensions in the model.

Once you've created this set of plans, begin communicating with your employees. Introduce the Employalty concept to your organization. Consider gifting copies of this book to introduce what is coming to hold your leadership group accountable. Tell your employees, "This book outlines the kind of employee experience we intend to build. You can count on us to make this a priority. We're counting on you to hold us accountable. After reading this book, please tell us where we're succeeding and where we're falling short." For some, it may make sense to take this step earlier, as part of your assessment phase, to create a fully transparent dialogue on what needs to change.

As part of your communication phase, invite contributors from all parts of the organization to take an active role in shaping some of the work you outlined in your 30-, 90-, and

180-day plans. Invite manager and non-manager employees to be part of project groups or committees with clear directives. Mine them for their feedback and listen to their recommendations. Along the way, keep the communication going with everyone in the company. Make everything you learn and plan to do available to your employees. If possible, implement those quick wins in your 30-day plan to demonstrate your commitment to improvement and to spark momentum for the transformation. In some places, this could have an immediate impact on retention and engagement.

As weeks turn to months and you execute on your three plans, periodically reassess and adjust plans accordingly to ensure you are actually improving the employee experience in each of the nine Employalty dimensions. During this phase of your work, encourage supervisors to start using the Employalty Scorecard as a diagnostic tool with individual employees. For high performers, find out what dimensions are most present and important to them, as well as any that might be lacking. This is a powerful way to actively nurture retention. For employees who may be underperforming, explore what's missing from their scorecard and consider whether these issues can be remedied. You can do this any time an employee is struggling or seems checked out. In this way, the Employalty Scorecard is the most powerful tool at your disposal to figure out why someone may not be thriving.

The clearest indicators to whether your organization is getting things right or wrong are applicants and turnover. Keep an eye on these numbers. If possible, break it down by position. If, for example, management positions have low turnover but sales associates are still hard to attract, you can begin tweaking the nine dimensions with regard to those specific positions. This enables you to respond in a targeted way to the market, role, and industry within which you are competing.

Remember, the people who run the Alabama football program constantly ask, "How do we make our program the best place in the country for college football players?" This is the question to ask if you're still struggling to fill or retain people in specific roles. If you own a car dealership and are struggling to fill sales positions, start with the question, "How do we make this place the best place in the world for someone to be a sales associate?" If you have a hard time keeping servers or wait staff at your restaurant, start asking, "How do we make this place the very best place in the region to be a server?" If you run a hotel and are short-staffed in the housekeeping department, ask the question, "For someone considering being a housekeeper, what would make our positions the best housekeeper roles in our area?"

These questions point you in a simple direction: figuring out how to make your positions incomparable to everyone else's. These questions force you to innovate. They force you to learn more about what people who fill these roles really want and need. These questions force you to do market research on pay and benefits and examine creative ways to adjust schedules or design roles. As part of your research, regularly ask the people who do these various jobs in your company what they'd change about their job if they could. Tell them everything is on the table. Ask for "pie in the sky" thinking. I bet you'll hear at least a few great ideas that aren't too hard to implement.

As you grow ever closer to creating the kind of employee experience that reflects all nine dimensions of the Employalty model, it's time to start using that to your advantage. Highlight the conditions you've worked to create for your employees. Share them in job postings, on your marketing channels, on social media, and with your vendors and business partners. Once you've put in the effort to make your company a great place to work, tell everyone. Talk about

Employalty to job candidates and clients. Say, "We are an Employalty workplace. We are committed to a more humane employee experience to prioritize your quality of life." Give this book to job candidates and clients as a promise of what they can expect by working with you. Make that promise proudly and reap all the benefits that come with creating a destination workplace.

Build Better Bosses

There is no debate that an employee's boss is the single most influential factor in the employee experience. Still, much needs to change to consistently fill workplaces with better bosses. To adjust to this new reality, companies must commit to prioritizing and protecting time for leaders to participate in ongoing learning. This kind of regular development work is among the most important ways a leader can spend their time. Everything else they do—and everything that you desire them to achieve—flows from it. Until you commit to intentional pre-role preparation and pair it with ongoing leadership development practices like training, coaching, and peer support programs, your chances at creating a destination workplace will remain low.

Making time for continuous learning and peer support is especially important for front-line managers. Sadly, though, these employee-facing supervisors are often lowest on the priority list when it comes to developmental targeting and resources. As someone who is contacted regularly to facilitate workshops, deliver training, or host deep-dive masterclasses with organizations, I've observed a pattern of companies more highly valuing executive development over management training. There is a more frequent willingness to part with financial resources to support senior leaders than those "in the field." It's sad, really, and should be the opposite. Front-line leaders have more influence on commitment in a company than anyone else. It's time we treated them that way.

After all, an employee's boss is the architect of their commitment. If an employee feels valued and seen (or not) it's because of how their boss operates. If the employee decides to trade their time, creativity, and maximum effort on behalf of their employer, it's because the environment created by their boss makes them believe it is worthwhile to do so. In fact, none of the advice and strategies outlined in this book can be executed without better bosses. The compensation, workload, and flexibility that make for Ideal Jobs is facilitated at the ground level by bosses. Nurturing purpose, aligning work with strengths, and cultivating belonging as outlined in the Meaningful Work section can truly *only* be done by an employee's boss. And the coaching, trust, and advocacy employees need to experience from a Great Boss must be taught and sustained.

So, again, you can't ignore this or do leadership development in half-measures. You have to have it. The good news is that the time needed to build better bosses does not always need to be in formal educational programming. In one study on effective managers, researchers found that among those leaders rated most highly by their employees, the most common factor is that those leaders were a part of *a peer group of managers*. They had a group of management colleagues with whom to debrief, discuss challenges, seek new ideas, or simply vent. Making sure that leaders in your organization are able to connect, discuss, and bond is an easy way to leverage this finding and benefit from it. For ultra-small organizations where just one or two people serve as a supervisor,

Employalty is the
evidence-based
framework for retaining
employees, unlocking
their commitment,
and leveling up your
company's performance.

———————

encouraging active participation in local business groups or professional trade associations can create similar experiences.

Remember, great employees follow Great Bosses, not just on the job, but out the door. Employees know how rare it is to work for someone who values them, treats them with respect, sees their talents, supports their creativity, and preserves their work-life boundaries. They know how much time it takes to earn mutual trust, prove yourself to those in charge, and become a valued member of a team. That's why so many great employees follow Great Bosses to other companies when those Great Bosses move on. Keep Great Bosses, and you'll keep great employees. Remember, everything outlined in this book applies to finding and keeping devoted *managers* too.

Spheres of Influence

I'd like to think there's a little something in this book for leaders at all levels. Whether you're a front-line supervisor, mid-level manager, director, VP, CEO, or business owner, understanding the experiences that lead employees to join an organization, stay long term, and contribute at a high level over time is key to your success as a leader. That said, your place on the "org chart" can limit your sphere of influence. This is the power you possess to effect change within your organization.

Not all leaders enjoy the same amount of influence. Front-line and mid-level leaders, for example, have limited influence over organizational policies, pay scales, and strategic priorities. Yet their proximity to individual contributors grants them more influence than anyone else on many of the essential components of our Employalty framework, like belonging, strengths, and coaching. At the same time, senior leaders in an organization are usually the only ones who can increase compensation, drive policies that create position flexibility, and prioritize the ongoing training and development leaders need to become Great Bosses.

As you work to create an Employalty movement in your organization, talk openly about your spheres of influence. Ask leaders across the organizational chart to identify the areas where they can take ownership and be held accountable for improvement. Ask those same leaders to identify the areas of the framework where they feel most powerless. Ensure that all nine dimensions of the framework have a champion in the organization, someone with the proper influence to truly create change in each area. Over time, an Employalty movement requires a partnership between those who lead on the front lines and those who control the resources and strategy of the organization. Like cogs in a complex machine, if one gear malfunctions, the whole mechanism goes kaput.

If you're reading this book as a front-line supervisor, be mindful of how easy it is to insist that the path to attracting and keeping talent revolves mostly around money. While it's true that in many (maybe even most) places, a significant increase in compensation can go a long way to improving both hiring and retention, money alone isn't the answer. Because money has a limited sphere of influence. Insisting only that we throw more money at employees lets you off the hook for everything else discussed in this book and the significant role it plays in the employee experience in the long term. There are plenty of high-paying jobs out there that companies are struggling to keep filled because they're failing to attend to the other dimensions of Employalty. Your employer may need to pay more, yes, but it's likely that you can do more, too, to ensure that the complete employee experience outlined in this book is happening for your team members. Look at the framework again. Are you using your sphere of influence to create a more personal, more humane employee experience?

Leaders aren't the only characters in our story that have differing spheres of influence. The three factors of Employalty—Ideal Job, Meaningful Work, and Great Boss—also have different spheres of influence. Collectively, I've argued that getting people to join an organization, stay long term, care about their work, and try hard each day are what transpires when the Employalty framework is successfully in place at a company. These four outcomes—*join*, *stay*, *care*, and *try*—are not all affected equally by the three factors of Employalty. Ideal Job, for example, has a much greater influence on *join* and *stay* and far less influence on *care* and *try*. This is because *join* and *stay* are greatly influenced by extrinsic motivators like pay, workload, and schedule. The three dimensions of Ideal Job—compensation, workload, and flexibility—play a huge role in getting candidates to *join* your organization and *stay* long term. If your biggest challenge is getting candidates to apply for open positions or accept job offers, you'll want to focus your efforts on the dimensions of Ideal Job as they are most critical to *attracting* candidates in this new age of work.

Once employees join your organization, however, the dimensions of Ideal Job become slightly less important than the other factors of Meaningful Work and Great Boss. That's because these two factors are key to triggering intrinsic motivation. This is the effort and energy people give to things they find interesting, fulfilling, and purposeful. When employees find their work inherently enjoyable and challenging in a good way, they become emotionally invested and deploy discretionary effort—they *care* and *try*. If your biggest challenge is turnover—you're struggling to keep employees after they've chosen to join the organization—you'll want to examine the experiences they're having in relation to Meaningful Work and Great Boss, as these have far greater influence on commitment over time, provided the dimensions of Ideal Job are satisfactorily met.

Square Pegs

I get asked often, "Do you believe every employee is capable of becoming a high performer?" My answer is always, "Yes, somewhere."

As we've explored in this book, we must challenge ourselves at times to question our beliefs about where work ethic comes from. For some leaders, there is the belief that you either have it or you don't. For others, there is the belief that work ethic is something that everyone can demonstrate if they are psychologically activated by the right combination of environment and circumstance. I'm part of the latter group. I believe nearly every person is capable of being a high-performing individual contributor somewhere. Part of our jobs as leaders is to figure out if that somewhere is here. It's our job to identify the emotional and psychological buttons that, when pushed in the right order, produce commitment.

If someone on your team displays little work ethic, go through the steps to figure out what's missing from that combination of environment and circumstance. Are they in the right role based on their knowledge, skills, experience, and interests? Are there aspects of the Employalty model that are lacking, like a sense of belonging or a manageable workload? Are they experiencing things in their personal life that are inhibiting their ability to bring their full energy and attention to their work? This is the exploration that must occur to ignite commitment when it appears to be lacking. Here again, that Employalty Scorecard becomes the diagnostic tool to help you troubleshoot that employee's experience.

However, if you've done all you can to create the conditions for the employee to thrive and they still don't, then your path forward is clear. You accept that, while this person has worth and talents, your organization is not the right fit for them. You accept that you've been trying to fit a square peg into a round hole. In these cases, the leader can empathetically deliver the message that "this place isn't the right fit for you." It's not that they're lazy, they don't care, or are a bad person. Instead of assuming a character defect, accept that they are a square peg and set them free to find a place with square holes while you go about the business of finding a round peg.

By the way, approaching people management with this mindset makes the act of terminating someone easier for all parties involved. When you release someone from an environment that isn't right for them, you very well may be putting them on to a path of more professional and personal happiness that results from them moving into a new role or new organization that is better suited to who they are. At the same time, since you are now a destination workplace, you can upgrade in that position with someone looking for the kind of employee experience your organization provides.

That's what happens when you commit to the Employalty model. A more humane employee experience, one that gives each person their Ideal Job, doing Meaningful Work, for a Great Boss, means your talent pool will grow. When your workforce is fulfilled, word of mouth spreads. Your employees become your best recruiters. While others suffer at jobs that lack crucial ingredients, your employees will trumpet the experience they have at work. They'll boast about the generous compensation, manageable workload, and flexibility that make their job ideal. They'll wax poetic about how meaningful their work is because they get to use their strengths in service to a purpose at a place where they belong. They'll rave about their boss, who they'll say trusts them, coaches them, and advocates for them. Instead of struggling to find applicants, you will have people lining up begging just to be considered for a spot in your company, which takes such extraordinary care of its people.

Experiences over Culture

From the first page of this book, I have tried as much as possible to avoid using the word "culture." Yes, it has shown up a few times. It's not because culture isn't important or doesn't matter. It's because, as a word, it's become chronically overused and underdefined. In too many places, leaders spend hours brainstorming in a conference room and come out with a set of special words that, at an intellectual level, reflects who they think they are or what they want to be about and declare it their culture. Most of the time these ideals don't actually exist. In these cases, they'll say they're *striving toward* this culture. Yet without fail, suddenly those words become "who we are" and "what we believe in" without doing any of the work to turn those special words into actual experiences lived by the people at every level of the organization.

In other words, most of the time, when you hear someone talk about their culture, they're really telling you about their fantasies. Without doing the work, defining culture is often akin to making a list of wishes. I talk with business owners and leaders every week who can't wait to tell me what their culture is and then ask for help fixing entrenched problems that wouldn't be there if that's what their culture really was.

My favorite definition of the word "culture" was coined by the authors Terrence Deal and Allan Kennedy way back in 1982. They said culture is "the way we do things around here."

This is often where the culture that leaders aspire to and the culture that actually exists collide. It's the difference between culture as a set of unfulfilled ideals and culture as a set of lived experiences. An organization can proclaim a culture of innovation, but if team members describe their ideas and requests being consistently dismissed due to costs or budget, it's actually a culture of cost-savings and restriction. When an employer proclaims a culture of respect, but refuses to list wages on job postings or ghosts candidates after interviews, they're actually living a culture of disrespect. A company can trumpet a culture of service, but if customers experience long wait times or curt interactions with employees, then that is the culture, not the special word printed on the mugs everyone got at the mandatory training last month.

This is why I've avoided talking about Employalty as a culture. It's not an ethereal concept. It's a collection of experiences. To successfully find and keep devoted employees, the people in your organization must *experience* their Ideal Job, doing Meaningful Work, for a Great Boss via the nine dimensions detailed in this book. These must be the experiences that consistently show up as a part of your team members' daily lives. These nine dimensions act like the individual wooden blocks in that popular stacking game Jenga. The more pieces you remove, the more unstable the structure becomes, until one too many pieces disappear and the whole thing falls apart.

When all the pieces are present, however, the structure is consistently strong and stable. As you work to start an Employalty movement in your organization, know that each of the dimensions outlined herein is important, but together, the whole is even greater than the sum of its parts.

15

The Blockbuster Epilogue

DESPITE BEING on the verge of bankruptcy, their only option was to rent a private jet.

The three executives had been requesting a meeting with the leadership at video rental giant Blockbuster for months. Their young company was in trouble. It was September 2000, and the dot-com crash coupled with slower-than-expected customer growth had pushed their company to the brink of collapse. The three leaders were convinced that a sale to Blockbuster was the best path to survival. These men were together in an evening meeting in California when they learned that Blockbuster had, finally, granted their request for a sit-down. The only problem?

Blockbuster wanted them in Dallas at 11:30 the next morning.

The three men—co-founders Marc Randolph and Reed Hastings, along with CFO Barry McCarthy—saw this for what it was: a power move. This was a *flex* designed to put them in their place. After all, they were competitors. The company these men built was trying to siphon business from Blockbuster with a DVD-rental-by-mail service they called Netflix. In his book *That Will Never Work*, Randolph recounted their meeting with Blockbuster in the fall of 2000 and the events leading up to it. When Hastings suggested that the only way they could make the meeting was to charter a private jet, CFO McCarthy objected, citing the $20,000 expense. Hastings replied, "We've waited months to get this meeting. We're on track to lose at least $50 million this year. Whether we pull this off or not, another twenty grand won't make a difference."

They booked the charter.

Around the table the next day were several members of Blockbuster's leadership team, but the visitors from Netflix knew theirs was an audience of one. CEO John Antioco had joined the company two years earlier, during a downturn in Blockbuster's performance, and was largely credited with turning things around. A year earlier, he'd presided over a successful IPO that raised $465 million for the company. As Randolph writes, "He was ready to hear us out, but what we said had better be good."

At the meeting, Hastings aimed to make the acquisition of Netflix a no-brainer value-add for Blockbuster. He efficiently detailed Blockbuster's strengths and identified areas where they could benefit from Netflix's market position and experience. He suggested that if Blockbuster bought Netflix, "we will run the online part of the combined business. You will focus on the stores. We will find the synergies that come from the combination, and it will truly be a case of the whole being greater than the sum of its parts."

The Blockbuster leadership team were dismissive. Their general counsel proclaimed that the business models of Netflix and nearly every other online business would never be profitable. The Netflix executives challenged these perceptions for a few minutes, then the question was asked: "If we were to buy you, what were you thinking? I mean, a number."

"Fifty million," Hastings said.

Randolph writes that during this discussion, he was watching Antioco. He notes that throughout the meeting the Blockbuster CEO was engaged and professional, demonstrating all the nonverbal cues of someone listening attentively. When Hastings quoted their price, however, Antioco's face changed. The corners of his mouth turned upward slightly. Randolph says it lasted only a moment, "but as soon as I saw it, I knew what was happening."

"John Antioco was struggling not to laugh."

You probably know that Blockbuster never bought Netflix. The meeting between the executive teams in 2000 never resulted in a sale, or even a serious counteroffer from Blockbuster. At the time, the leadership of the video rental company couldn't imagine a future that existed entirely online or that didn't include the ritual of going to the video store and browsing the titles available to rent.* Turning down the chance to buy Netflix for $50 million will go down as one of the great business gaffes of all time. It's one mistake in a series of errors made by Blockbuster that ultimately led to its demise.

Not long after that fall 2000 meeting, both companies found themselves facing an adapt-or-die moment. One knew it and changed how they did business: Netflix went from renting movies by mail to streaming. Blockbuster, conversely, was either oblivious to the future or resisted it for far too long. In its final years, Blockbuster tried to change, haphazardly embracing DVD-by-mail, streaming, and video on demand,

---

* If you were born after 1998, it's likely you have no connection to this experience.

but it was too late. The media giant went from having more than nine thousand stores worldwide to just one. Today, a single Blockbuster remains, a privately owned store in Bend, Oregon, its continued existence driven largely by nostalgia. Otherwise, the company no longer exists.

While Blockbuster went bankrupt in 2010, Netflix is now one of the world's most valuable companies. The streaming service currently has a market cap of $100 billion, or two thousand times the $50 million asking price floated at the meeting that day.

The Netflix-Blockbuster story is a lesson in what happens when you do or do not adjust to a changing business landscape. Just a few years ago, a massive disruption took place in how people wanted to consume entertainment. It happened quickly, because once the market saw what was possible (streaming) they wanted only that. Those who clung to the old way of doing business are no longer doing business.

Many employers are facing a similar adapt-or-die moment right now, as they struggle to find and keep people. After years of overwork and dehumanization, employees have gotten a glimpse of what's possible as some companies started engineering a better, more humane employee experience. Now that more and more workers are seeing a new way of working, they want only that, and those who cling to the old way of doing business are struggling to do business.

Your organization has a choice to make about its identity. Who do you want to be, Blockbuster or Netflix? As we've learned again and again in business, you must adapt to your market to remain relevant and viable. Now and into the future, will you be the departure organization or the destination workplace? If you want to find and keep devoted employees, unlock their commitment, and take your company's performance to the next level, the choice is clear.

Employalty isn't altruism.
It's a business strategy.
It's the new cost of doing
business well. It's the
entry fee for success.

———————————

Employalty is an identity you choose and a path you follow. It's an evidence-based framework you can use to overcome an entrenched, interconnected set of problems. Employalty isn't a gimmick or a cute play on words. It's a set of beliefs you hold and experiences you create to achieve the results you desire.

Companies that embrace Employalty understand that commitment is a two-way street. If we expect people to devote their time, attention, and effort to meeting our company's needs every day, we must devote ourselves to meeting our employees' needs every day. If this sounds transactional, that's because it is, at first. Once that transaction is equitable for both sides, however, the relationship becomes transformational for all parties involved. When employees love what they do, how they do it, and who they do it with and for, their health, well-being, and quality of life soar. They respond to these conditions with emotional and psychological commitment, which can produce astounding results for your business.

Remember, people will *do* the best job possible when they feel they *have* the best job possible.

Commit to them, and they'll commit to you.

As you journey forth, know that putting this framework into action in your company will take courage, time, and resources. But know, too, that your approach is sound and your cause is righteous. After all, you're operating in the best interest of your organization *and* the people you employ. By upgrading your employee experience, you will have a direct impact on the professional fulfillment and quality of life for everyone in your charge. Think about how rare that is. How many people truly love what they do or where they work? How many people dread going to work each day, return home miserable, and suffer that experience again and again?

Imagine the incredible social, physical, and mental health improvements that would take place across society if we made work *work* for more people.

You have that power.

And now you have the instruction manual.

It's time to get to work.

Acknowledgments

WASN'T SURE I was going to do this again.

At the end of my book *No More Team Drama: Ending the Gossip, Cliques, & Other Crap That Damage Workplace Teams*, I wrote about how difficult the process of writing is for me. While some aspects of this experience were much more enjoyable than the last, this was still a grueling marathon at times. I owe deep gratitude to a significant number of people for getting me across the finish line in possession of my sanity *and* a book I'm quite proud of.

I am blessed to have a network of friends and acquaintances much smarter than I, many of whom selflessly joined me in conversation about many aspects of this book. From the title to the premise, to the framework you just read about, these brilliant people all made this book better in one way or another. My sincerest thanks to Bruce Turkel, Laurie Guest, Jay Baer, Mark Levy, Neen James, Ron Tite, Caleb Gardner, and Dorie Clark.

I also owe immense thanks to each of the people who agreed to be interviewed for this book. Without question, my favorite part of writing *Employalty* was getting to sit with each of you, hear your words, and then tell your stories. I thank you for your courage, your vulnerability, and your trust in me to share your experiences with an audience. This book is but a pamphlet without your contributions.

To the terrific team at Page Two: Thank you for helping take this book from concept to reality. Every person I've worked with there has been gracious, wise, and devoted. A special and sincere thanks to James Harbeck, whose guidance as an editor was always warm, helpful, and thoughtful. Thank you for encouraging me to "just keep doing what you're doing" right from the start.

Thank you, Jamie DeRosa, for all the ways you contributed to this book, which are more than can be listed. From talking through ideas to keeping Joe Mull & Associates going during all the times I had to steal away to write without interruption, I couldn't have done it without you. Thanks for being such an outstanding outfielder.

My greatest thanks go to Jessica. When I told my wife of sixteen years that I decided to write another book, she didn't hesitate to offer her unabashed support. She did this knowing that, on top of being away regularly because of my travels as a speaker and trainer, I'd be spending many, many hours holed up or away to get writing done. As usual and without complaint, Jess selflessly ran our lives, working one seventeen-hour day after another, juggling her work, three kids, lots of soccer practices, and a high-strung Dalmatian named Flash. There is simply no way this book could have been written without having such a world-class partner. Thank you, darling.

Each of the people above contributed in one way or another to all the parts of this book that work or that you found useful. If you encountered anything you perceive to be a mistake, an absurdity, or an error in judgment, these are my fault alone. I'm sure they are in there. I hope they are rare.

Thank you for reading and for the privilege of your attention. It's something I aspire to never take for granted.

Notes

Numerals indicate page numbers where referenced text is found.

Chapter 1: Where Does Commitment Come From at Work?

6   *The biggest worker shortages are expected:* Roy Maurer, "The Biggest Future Employment Crisis: A Lack of Workers," SHRM, October 19, 2021, shrm.org/resourcesandtools/hr-topics/talent-acquisition/pages/the-biggest-future-employment-crisis-a-lack-of-workers.aspx; Bureau of Labor Statistics, "Employment Projections—2021–2031," US Department of Labor, news release, September 8, 2022, https://www.bls.gov/news.release/pdf/ecopro.pdf.

Chapter 2: Becoming a Destination Workplace

19   *Gallup found that the team leader alone: State of the American Manager: Analytics and Advice for Leaders,* Gallup poll report, 2015, gallup.com/services/182138/state-american-manager.aspx.

Chapter 3: The Breaking and Upgrading of Work

37   *Just a few months into the pandemic:* Eleanor Cummins, "Welcome to Covid-19's 'Junior Year.' It's Not Pretty," *Vox,* December 27, 2021, vox.com/22850742/omicron-covid-junior-year-resignation-fatigue-depression.

38   *The World Health Organization defines burnout as:* "Burn-Out an 'Occupational Phenomenon': International Classification of Diseases," World Health Organization, May 28, 2019, who.int/news/item/28-05-2019-burn-out-an-occupational-phenomenon-international-classification-of-diseases.

38　*77 percent of employees reported feeling burned out:* Ben Wigert and
Sangeeta Agrawal, "Employee Burnout, Part 1: The 5 Main Causes,"
Gallup, July 12, 2018, gallup.com/workplace/237059/employee-
burnout-part-main-causes.aspx.

38　*just months into the pandemic:* Jen Fisher, "Workplace Burnout
Survey: Burnout without Borders," Deloitte, www2.deloitte.com/us/
en/pages/about-deloitte/articles/burnout-survey.html.

38　*three out of five workers reported negative impacts:* Ashley Abramson,
"Burnout and Stress Are Everywhere," American Psychological
Association *2022 Trends Report* 53, no. 1 (January 1, 2022): 72,
apa.org/monitor/2022/01/special-burnout-stress.

38　*the American Psychological Association proclaimed that:* Abramson,
"Burnout and Stress Are Everywhere."

41　*In Australia, a nationally representative poll:* Paul Karp, "Australians
Working 1.5 Hours More Unpaid Overtime Each Week
Compared with Pre-Covid," *The Guardian*, November 16, 2021,
theguardian.com/australia-news/2021/nov/17/australians-working-
15-hours-more-unpaid-overtime-each-week-compared-to-pre-covid.

41　*In the UK, British workers toil:* "British Workers Putting In Longest
Hours in the EU, TUC Analysis Finds," Trades Union Congress,
April 17, 2019, tuc.org.uk/news/british-workers-putting-longest-
hours-eu-tuc-analysis-finds.

41　*Americans work hundreds of hours a year:* "Americans Work Longest
Hours among Industrialized Countries, Japanese Second Longest.
Europeans Work Less Time, but Register Faster Productivity Gains—
New ILO Statistical Volume Highlights Labour Trends Worldwide,"
International Labour Organization press release, September 6, 1999,
ilo.org/global/about-the-ilo/newsroom/news/WCMS_071326/
lang--en/index.htm.

42　*In nearly every other industrialized nation:* Adewale Maye,
"No-Vacation Nation, Revised," Center for Economic and Policy
Research, May 2019, cepr.net/images/stories/reports/no-vacation-
nation-2019-05.pdf.

42　*only 44 percent of American workers:* "Paid Time Off Trends
in the U.S.," U.S. Travel Association fact sheet, 2019,
ustravel.org/sites/default/files/media_root/document/
Paid%20Time%20Off%20Trends%20Fact%20Sheet.pdf.

43　*number of direct reports per manager increased: State of the American
Manager: Analytics and Advice for Leaders*, Gallup poll report, 2015,
gallup.com/services/182138/state-american-manager.aspx.

43 *two out of three workers reported being burned out:* Bryan Robinson,
    "Two-Thirds of Workers Experienced Burnout This Year:
    How to Reverse the Trend in 2020," *Forbes*, December 8, 2019,
    forbes.com/sites/bryanrobinson/2019/12/08/two-thirds-of-workers-
    experienced-burnout-this-year-how-to-reverse-the-trend-in-2020.

43 *In 2021, Americans quit their jobs in record numbers:* "Job Openings
    and Labor Turnover Survey," US Bureau of Labor Statistics,
    https://www.bls.gov/jlt/.

44 *The UK saw an all-time high of one million job vacancies:*
    Elizabeth Howlett, "Job Vacancies Hit All-Time High of Almost
    One Million, Official Figures Show," People Management,
    August 17, 2021, peoplemanagement.co.uk/article/1747259/
    job-vacancies-hit-all-time-high-one-million-official-figures-show.

44 *In Germany, more than 40 percent of companies:* Abi Carter,
    "Germany's Skilled Worker Shortage Reaches New Heights,"
    I Am Expat, June 6, 2022, iamexpat.de/career/employment-news/
    germanys-skilled-worker-shortage-reaches-new-heights.

44 *A slew of polls released in 2021 and into 2022:* Grace Dean and
    Madison Hoff, "Nearly Three-Quarters of Workers Are Actively
    Thinking about Quitting Their Job, According to a Recent
    Survey," *Business Insider*, October 17, 2021, businessinsider.com/
    great-resignation-labor-shortage-workers-thinking-about-quitting-
    joblist-report-2021-10.

45 *Klotz told* Business Insider *later that year:* Juliana Kaplan,
    "The Psychologist Who Coined the Phrase 'Great Resignation'
    Reveals How He Saw It Coming and Where He Sees It Going.
    'Who We Are as an Employee and as a Worker Is Very Central
    to Who We Are.'" *Business Insider*, October 2, 2021,
    businessinsider.com/why-everyone-is-quitting-great-resignation-
    psychologist-pandemic-rethink-life-2021-10.

46 *Job Openings and Labor Turnover Survey (JOLTS):* "Job Openings,
    Hires, and Separations Levels, Seasonally Adjusted," US Bureau
    of Labor Statistics, Graphics for Economic News Releases,
    https://www.bls.gov/charts/job-openings-and-labor-turnover/
    opening-hire-seps-level.htm.

47 *call the trend the Great* Upgrade: Juliana Kaplan and Madison Hoff,
    "A White House Economist Says It's a 'Great Upgrade,' Not a Great
    Resignation, as Workers Quit for Higher Pay," *Business Insider*,
    January 10, 2022, businessinsider.com/white-house-economist-
    great-upgrade-not-great-resignation-labor-shortage-2022-1.

47 *one out of every three workers would quit by 2023:* Thomas Mahan, Danny Nelms, Jeeun Yi, Alexander Jackson, Michael Hein, and Richard Moffett, *2020 Retention Report: Insights on 2019 Turnover Trends, Reasons, Costs & Recommendations*, Work Institute, 2020, info.workinstitute.com/hubfs/2020%20Retention%20Report/ Work%20Institutes%202020%20Retention%20Report.pdf.

49 *"I've never met a single person:* Brené Brown quoted in *Brené Brown: The Call to Courage*, directed by Sandra Restrepo, Netflix, 2019.

Chapter 4: Rehumanization and the Myth of Lazy

53 *laid off nine hundred employees all at once:* Emma Goldberg, "Better.com's C.E.O. 'Taking Time Off' after Firing 900 Workers over Zoom," *New York Times*, December 10, 2021, nytimes.com/ 2021/12/10/business/economy/better-ceo-zoom-firing.html.

53 *The fired workers shared their stunning experience:* Ramishah Maruf, "'A Surreal Moment': Fired Employees Share What It Was Like on That Mass-Firing Zoom," CNN Business, December 8, 2021, cnn.com/2021/12/07/business/better-zoom-firing-employees/ index.html.

53 *In comments to CBC radio, Christian Chapman:* "'It Was Callous,' Says Man Laid Off with 900 Employees on Zoom Call," *As It Happens*, CBC Radio, December 7, 2021, cbc.ca/radio/ asithappens/as-it-happens-the-tuesday-edition-1.6276506/ it-was-callous-says-man-laid-off-with-900-employees-on-zoom-call-1.6276956.

55 *Sephora laid off more than three thousand employees:* Shoshy Ciment, "A Sephora Employee Describes the Devastating Moment She and Others in Her District Were Suddenly Laid Off Via a Conference Call," *Business Insider*, April 1, 2020, businessinsider.com/ sephora-fires-employees-via-sudden-conference-call-2020-4.

55 *One month later, WW International:* Julie Creswell, "Mass Firing on Zoom Is Latest Sign of Weight Watchers Unrest," *New York Times*, June 11, 2020, nytimes.com/2020/05/22/business/ weight-watchers-firings-zoom.html.

55 *Williams-Sonoma did nearly the exact same thing:* Divya Kishore, "Outrage after Williams-Sonoma FIRES over 100 workers on Group Zoom Call before Christmas," Meaww, December 23, 2021, meaww.com/williams-sonoma-fires-over-100-workers-over-group-zoom-call-on-christmas-week.

57   *According to Dr. Karen Fiorini:* All quotes and notes from
Dr. Fiorini in this chapter are from her dissertation: Karen Fiorini,
"Dehumanization in the Workplace," PhD dissertation, Simon Fraser
University, March 8, 2019, theses.lib.sfu.ca/file/thesis/5234.

58   *executive at an Applebee's restaurant franchise chain:* Minda Zetlin,
"An Applebee's Exec Just Sent an Email That the Company Was
Quick to Disavow," *Inc.*, March 27, 2022, inc.com/minda-zetlin/
applebees-wayne-pankratz-email-reddit-gas-prices-lower-wages.html.

63   *unemployment in the US is below 4 percent:* Hillary Hoffower,
"Biden's Unemployment Numbers Are Lower Than Any Time
between the '70s and 2019, but He's Getting Slammed over
Expensive Gas," *Fortune*, June 3, 2022, fortune.com/2022/06/03/
joe-biden-unemployment-inflation-may-jobs-report-gas-prices/.

63   *The labor force participation rate:* Audrey Breitwieser,
Ryan Nunn, and Jay Shambaugh, "The Recent Rebound in
Prime-Age Labor Force Participation," Brookings, August 2, 2018,
brookings.edu/blog/up-front/2018/08/02the-recent-rebound-in-
prime-age-labor-force-participation/.

63   *"maybe people don't want to work for you":* Chris Westfall,
"'No One Wants to Work': The Why behind the Great Resignation,"
Forbes, January 19, 2022, forbes.com/sites/chriswestfall/
2022/01/19/no-one-wants-to-workthe-why-behind-the-great-
resignation/?sh=635057f072d7.

66   *documented the history of this phrase:* Paul Fairie (@paulisci),
Twitter thread, "A Brief History of Nobody Wants to Work
Anymore," July 19, 2022, 6:52 p.m., twitter.com/paulisci/
status/1549527748950892544.

Chapter 5: Compensation

73   *Sean Goode would sleep in his car:* Carla Bell, "One Nonprofit's
Motive for a $70K Minimum Salary? Employee Safety," *HR Dive*,
February 3, 2022, hrdive.com/news/one-nonprofits-motive-for-a-
70k-minimum-salary-employee-safety/618223/.

74   *he did not see the raises as necessary:* Hanna Scott, "Workers at
Seattle Nonprofit Just Got a $20,000 Raise, and We Should All Pay
Attention," *MyNorthwest*, November 15, 2021, mynorthwest.com/
3239003/seattle-nonprofit-choose-180-raise-70000-salary/.

74   *the threshold to meet basic needs:* Massachusetts Institute of
Technology (MIT), "Living Wage Calculator," livingwage.mit.edu.

75 *To get employees to a minimum $70,000:* Naomi Ishisaka, "A King County Nonprofit Raised All Staff Salaries to $70,000 Minimum. Will More Organizations Follow?" *Seattle Times*, November 15, 2021, seattletimes.com/seattle-news/labor-shortage-or-living-wage-shortage-one-king-county-nonprofit-is-taking-a-different-approach/.

77 *regional costs of living in the US can vary widely:* Andy Kiersz, "RANKED: All 50 States and DC, from Least to Most Average," *Business Insider*, October 12, 2016, businessinsider.com/average-state-ranking-2016-10.

77 *Add a child, and that worker needs to earn:* MIT, "Living Wage Calculator."

78 *According to the Economic Policy Institute:* John Schmitt, Elise Gould, and Josh Bivens, "America's Slow-Motion Wage Crisis," Economic Policy Institute, September 13, 2018, epi.org/publication/americas-slow-motion-wage-crisis-four-decades-of-slow-and-unequal-growth-2/.

78 *A dollar today only buys 25 percent:* Ian Webster, "Value of $1 from 1979 to 2022," CPI Inflation Calculator, in2013dollars.com/us/inflation/1979?amount=1.

78 *Adjusted for inflation, the typical male worker:* Paul Krugman, "The Revolt of the American Worker," *New York Times*, October 14, 2021, nytimes.com/2021/10/14/opinion/workers-quitting-wages.html; FRED Economic Data, "Employed Full Time: Median Usual Weekly Real Earnings: Wage and Salary Workers: 16 Years and Over: Men," Economic Research, fred.stlouisfed.org/series/LES1252881900Q.

78 *people of color face the lowest pay:* Courtney Connley, "Why Black Workers Still Face a Promotion and Wage Gap That's Costing the Economy Trillions," CNBC, April 16, 2021, cnbc.com/2021/04/16/black-workers-face-promotion-and-wage-gaps-that-cost-the-economy-trillions.html.

78 *Black women, who face both gender and racial barriers:* Elise Gould and Valerie Wilson, "Black Workers Face Two of the Most Lethal Preexisting Conditions for Coronavirus—Racism and Economic Inequality," Economic Policy Institute, June 1, 2020, epi.org/publication/black-workers-covid/.

78 *paltry wage gains of the last four decades:* Drew Desilver, "For Most U.S. Workers, Real Wages Have Barely Budged in Decades," Pew Research Center, August 7, 2018, pewresearch.org/fact-tank/2018/08/07/for-most-us-workers-real-wages-have-barely-budged-for-decades/.

79   *The highest raises—10 percent:* Lisa Rowan, "57% of Americans Say Their Pay Raises Aren't Keeping Up with Inflation," *Forbes*, March 16, 2022, forbes.com/advisor/personal-finance/pay-raises-dont-match-high-inflation/.

79   *EPI estimates that since 1978:* Lawrence Mishel and Jori Kandra, "CEO Pay Has Skyrocketed 1,322% since 1978," Economic Policy Institute, August 10, 2021, epi.org/publication/ceo-pay-in-2020/.

79   *One in eight adults and one in six kids:* Monica Hake, Adam Dewey, Emily Engelhard, Mark Strayer, Sena Dawes, Tom Summerfelt, and Craig Gundersen, "The Impact of the Coronavirus on Food Insecurity in 2020 & 2021," Feeding America, March 2021, feedingamerica.org/sites/default/files/2021-03/National%20Projections%20Brief_3.9.2021_0.pdf.

79   *One in ten Americans have no health insurance:* Amy Cha and Robin Cohen, "Demographic Variation in Health Insurance Coverage: United States, 2020," Centers for Disease Control and Prevention *National Health Statistics Reports*, no. 169, February 11, 2022, cdc.gov/nchs/data/nhsr/nhsr169.pdf.

79   *In 2020, the average cost of rent:* Irina Lupa, "RentCafe National Rent Report: The Average Apartment Rent Was $1,468 in February," RentCafe, March 16, 2020, rentcafe.com/blog/rental-market/apartment-rent-report/february-2020-national-rent-report/.

79   *putting a baby in a licensed childcare facility:* Claire Suddath, "How Child Care Became the Most Broken Business in America," Bloomberg, November 18, 2021, bloomberg.com/news/features/2021-11-18/biden-s-build-back-better-wants-to-save-america-s-child-care-business.

80   *58 percent of Americans live paycheck to paycheck:* Jessica Dickler, "58% of Americans Are Living Paycheck to Paycheck after Inflation Spike—Including 30% of Those Earning $250,000 or More," CNBC, June 27, 2022, cnbc.com/2022/06/27/more-than-half-of-americans-live-paycheck-to-paycheck-amid-inflation.html.

80   *40 percent of Americans are one paycheck away from homelessness:* Kasey Wiedrich and David Newville, "Vulnerability in the Face of Economic Uncertainty: Findings from the 2019 *Prosperity Now ScoreCard*," *Prosperity Now ScoreCard*, January 2019, prosperitynow.org/sites/default/files/resources/2019_Scorecard_Key_Findings.pdf.

80   *Wages are staggeringly behind:* Larry Mishel and Nick Hanauer, "Wage Suppression—Not Stagnation—Is Costing Workers $10 an Hour," *The Hill*, June 10, 2021, thehill.com/opinion/finance/557798-wage-suppression-not-stagnation-is-costing-workers-10-an-hour/; Lawrence Mishel and Josh Bivens, "Identifying the Policy Levers Generating Wage Suppression and Wage Inequality," Economic Policy Institute, May 13, 2021, epi.org/unequalpower/publications/wage-suppression-inequality/.

81   *most notably health insurance:* Schmitt et al., "America's Slow-Motion Wage Crisis."

81   *As the former president of the EPI wrote:* Mishel and Hanauer, "Wage Suppression."

82   *Bank of America, the second largest bank in the US:* Kate Gibson, "Bank of America Hikes Its U.S. Minimum Wage to $21 an Hour," Living Wage, October 8, 2021, livingwage.mit.edu/articles/87-bank-of-america-hikes-its-u-s-minimum-wage-to-21-an-hour.

82   *US wireless carrier Verizon Communications:* "Verizon Raises Minimum Wage to $20 an Hour for U.S. Employees," Reuters, April 18, 2022, reuters.com/business/verizon-raises-minimum-wage-20-an-hour-us-employees-2022-04-18/.

82   *KLLM—a large US trucking firm:* Breck Dumas, "Trucking Company Enacts Largest Pay Increase in History," Fox Business, January 22, 2022, foxbusiness.com/economy/trucking-company-enacts-largest-pay-increase-in-company-history.

82   *Amid the Great Resignation, Morgan Stanley:* Jason Lalljee and Ben Winck, "It's Time for Corporate Profits to Return to the '90s so Companies Can Make Up for Decades of Underpaying Workers, Morgan Stanley Says," *Business Insider*, December 1, 2021, businessinsider.com/corporate-profits-drop-lift-worker-pay-morgan-stanley-labor-shortage-2021-12.

82   *literature on the psychology of motivation reveals:* Daniel H. Pink, *Drive: The Surprising Truth about What Motivates Us* (New York: Riverhead Books, 2009).

83   *generous pay to employees often results in:* Zeynep Ton, *The Good Jobs Strategy: How the Smartest Companies Invest in Employees to Lower Costs and Boost Profits* (Boston: New Harvest, Houghton Mifflin Harcourt, 2014).

84   *Employee turnover at PayPal:* Shannen Balogh, "PayPal Workers
     Were Struggling to Make Ends Meet; CEO Dan Schulman
     Vowed to Change That," SHRM, October 4, 2021, shrm.org/
     executive/resources/articles/pages/paypal-ceo-helps-workers-
     with-finances.aspx.

84   *In 2015, payment processing firm Gravity Payments:* "CEO on
     Why Giving All Employees Minimum Salary of $70,000
     Still 'Works' Six Years Later: 'Our Turnover Rate Was Cut in
     Half,'" CBS News, September 16, 2021, cbsnews.com/news/
     dan-price-gravity-payments-ceo-70000-employee-minimum-wage/.

84   *Gravity Payments now receives about 25,000 job applications:*
     Stephen Silver, "Gravity Payments' Dan Price on Why Raising
     Employee Salaries Works," DealerScope, March 22, 2022,
     dealerscope.com/2022/03/sxsw-2022-gravity-payments-founder-
     dan-price-why-raising-employee-salaries-works/.

85   *In one study, a $1.00 increase in hourly wages:* Zeynep Ton,
     "Why 'Good Jobs' Are Good for Retailers," *Harvard Business Review*,
     January–February 2012, hbr.org/2012/01/why-good-jobs-are-
     good-for-retailers.

85   *According to the Society for Human Resource Management:*
     Elliott Brown, "Exclusive Survey Data: Which Benefits
     Do Employees Want Most?" OnPay, June 9, 2022, onpay.com/
     benefits/guide/benefits-employees-want.

85   *In addition to raising their base pay:* Rina Torchinsky, "Target Is
     Raising Its Minimum Wage to as Much as $24 an Hour," NPR,
     March 1, 2022, npr.org/2022/03/01/1083720431/target-
     minimum-wage.

85   *At Dick's Drive-In, a West Coast burger chain:* Rachel Belle, "How
     Does Dick's Drive-In Pay Workers $19 an Hour with a Menu
     Completely under $5?" KIRO Newsradio, October 5, 2021,
     mynorthwest.com/3177050/how-does-dicks-drive-in-pay-workers-
     19-an-hours/.

86   *Wharton professor and organizational psychologist:* Adam
     Grant, "Why It Pays More to Pay More: Transcript," *WorkLife
     with Adam Grant*, May 11, 2021, ted.com/podcasts/worklife/
     why-it-pays-more-to-pay-more-transcript.

87   *must think of employees not as costs, but as assets:* Ton, *The Good
     Jobs Strategy.*

88 *one-half to two times an employee's salary to replace that person:*
Shane McFeely and Ben Wigert, "This Fixable Problem Costs
U.S. Businesses $1 Trillion," Gallup, March 13, 2019, gallup.com/
workplace/247391/fixable-problem-costs-businesses-trillion.aspx.

Chapter 6: Workload

100 *Americans now spend up to 19 percent more time on the job:* Alexander
Bick, Bettina Brüggemann, and Nicola Fuchs-Schündeln, "Hours
Worked in Europe and the US: New Data, New Answers," IZA,
Discussion Paper No. 10179, August 2016, docs.iza.org/dp10179.pdf.

100 *The average office worker receives 120 emails:* Radica Boshnjakoska,
"How Many Emails Are Sent per Day?" Review 42, review42.com/
resources/how-many-emails-are-sent-per-day/?gclid=COa3j-
bOkZgCFRg6awodKWCXmQ//////.

100 *An analysis of the emails and meetings:* Danielle Kost, "You're Right!
You Are Working Longer and Attending More Meetings,"
Harvard Business School Working Knowledge, September 14, 2020,
hbswk.hbs.edu/item/you-re-right-you-are-working-longer-and-
attending-more-meetings.

100 *workaholics are now common among nineteen-to-thirty-five-year-old
workers:* Katie Johnston, "Millennials Aren't Lazy, They're
Workaholics," *Boston Globe*, December 19, 2016, bostonglobe.com/
business/2016/12/19/millennials-aren-lazy-they-workaholics/
3ZD86pLBYg954qUEYa3SUJ/story.html.

100 *One research team that looked at long work hours:* Frank Pega,
Bálint Náfrádi, Natalie C. Momen, Yuka Ujita, Kai N. Streichera,
Annette M. Prüss-Üstüna, et al., "Global, Regional, and National
Burdens of Ischemic Heart Disease and Stroke Attributable to
Exposure to Long Working Hours for 194 Countries, 2000–2016:
A Systematic Analysis from the WHO/ILO Joint Estimates of
the Work-Related Burden of Disease and Injury," *Environment
International* 154, September 2021, doi.org/10.1016/j.envint
.2021.106595.

101 *According to the Centers for Disease Control and Prevention:*
Claire C. Caruso, Edward M. Hitchcock, Robert B. Dick,
John M. Russo, Jennifer M. Schmit, "Overtime and Extended Work
Shifts: Recent Findings on Illnesses, Injuries, and Health Behaviors,"
US Department of Health and Human Services, Centers for
Disease Control and Prevention, National Institute for Occupational
Safety and Health, April 2004, cdc.gov/niosh/docs/2004-143/
pdfs/2004-143.pdf.

103 *Between 2015 and 2019, Iceland ran a series of trials:* Paulina Villegas
      and Hannah Knowles, "Iceland Tested a 4-Day Workweek.
      Employees Were Productive—and Happier, Researchers
      Say," *Washington Post*, July 7, 2021, washingtonpost.com/
      business/2021/07/06/iceland-four-day-work-week/.

103 *Workers also reported less stress at home:* "Four-Day Week
      'an Overwhelming Success' in Iceland," BBC News, July 6, 2021,
      bbc.com/news/business-57724779.

103 *Now, 86 percent of Iceland's workforce:* Villegas and Knowles,
      "Iceland Tested a 4-Day Workweek."

104 *The Spanish government agreed to:* Jack Kelly, "Spain Is the Latest
      Country to Try a 4-Day Workweek," *Forbes*, March 15, 2021,
      forbes.com/sites/jackkelly/2021/03/15/spain-is-the-latest-country-
      to-try-a-four-day-workweek/?sh=151bae5af1da.

104 *all announced plans to explore a reduced workweek:* Warda Imran,
      "Working Four Days a Week: Hit or Miss?" DW, September 5, 2021,
      dw.com/en/four-day-work-week-a-mixed-success/a-59091672.

104 *Denmark, which consistently ranks among the top three happiest
      countries:* World Happiness Report, worldhappiness.report.

104 *InDebted, a debt collection agency:* Josh Foreman, "We Moved to
      a 4-Day Workweek Last Year. Here's How It's Going,"
      Fast Company, January 6, 2022, fastcompany.com/90710679/
      we-moved-to-a-4-day-workweek-last-year-heres-how-its-going.

104 *embraced by Bolt, an ecommerce developer:* Roula Amire, "Bolt's 4-Day
      Workweek Boosts Employee Happiness and Well-Being," Great
      Place to Work, May 5, 2022, greatplacetowork.com/resources/blog/
      bolt's-4-day-workweek-boosts-employee-happiness-and-well-being.

105 *all currently testing or offering a four-day workweek:* Giulia
      Carbonaro, "Every U.S. Company with a 4-Day Workweek—
      Full List," *Newsweek*, April 20, 2022, newsweek.com/
      every-us-company-4-day-workweek-full-list-1697943.

105 *Joe O'Connor, Global Pilot Program Manager at 4 Day Week Global:*
      Michelle Fox, "This Company Just Decided to Give Employees
      a 4-Day Workweek Permanently," CNBC, January 5, 2022,
      cnbc.com/2022/01/05/the-4-day-workweek-becomes-permanent-
      for-tech-company-bolt.html.

105 *Happiness expert Dan Buettner has reviewed research:* Karla Hult,
      "Are You Happy? 11 Steps to a Happier Life," KARE11,
      April 30, 2018, kare11.com/article/entertainment/television/
      programs/kare-11-extras/are-you-happy-11-steps-to-a-happier-life/
      89-547374405.

105 *even shaving an hour or two off:* Andrew Merle, "This Is the Optimal Number of Hours You Should Work Every Day," *Fast Company*, September 3, 2021, fastcompany.com/90671494/ this-is-the-optimal-number-of-hours-you-should-work-every-day.

107 *those who are overburdened with work tend to:* Stephen Casner and Brian Gore, *Measuring and Evaluating Workload: A Primer*, NASA, Ames Research Center report, July 2010, matb-files.larc.nasa.gov/ Workload_Primer_TM_Final.pdf.

108 *Using instruments such as the NASA Task Load Index:* "Workload Assessment," US Department of Transportation Federal Railroad Administration, October 25, 2019, railroads.dot.gov/human-factors/ elearning-attention/workload-assessment.

108 *In jobs where employees experience even short breaks:* Diana Yates, "Brief Diversions Vastly Improve Focus, Researchers Find," Illinois News Bureau, February 8, 2011, news.illinois.edu/view/ 6367/205427.

Chapter 7: Flexibility

120 *Flexibility is now the most sought-after work benefit:* HR Q&As, "What Benefits Can Employers Offer to Improve Employee Retention?" SHRM, shrm.org/resourcesandtools/tools-and-samples/ hr-qa/pages/benefits-to-improve-employee-retention.aspx.

120 *a flexible schedule is now more important:* Megan Leonhardt, "Employers Are Upping Pay and Benefits to Keep Workers from Resigning. Here Are the Perks Workers Want Most," *Fortune*, February 23, 2022, fortune.com/2022/02/23/employers-increasing- pay-benefits-workers/.

120 *up to 80 percent of companies:* Jessica Howington, "80% of Companies Offer Flexible Work Options," FlexJobs, flexjobs.com/blog/ post/80-companies-offer-flexible-work-options/.

120 *In a survey of nearly a quarter of a million workers:* Rainer Strack, Orsolya Kovács-Ondrejkovic, Jens Baier, Pierre Antebi, Kate Kavanagh, and Ana López Gobernado, "Decoding Global Ways of Working," Boston Consulting Group, March 31, 2021, bcg.com/ en-us/publications/2021/advantages-of-remote-work-flexibility.

125 *Microsoft CEO Satya Nadella said:* Jared Spataro, "2 Years of Digital Transformation in 2 Months," Microsoft Malaysia News Center, May 4, 2020, news.microsoft.com/en-my/2020/05/04 /2-years-of-digital-transformation-in-2-months/.

Chapter 8: Purpose

134 *when we perceive our work as being worthwhile, important, or valued:*
Blake A. Allan, Cassondra Batz-Barbarich, Haley M. Sterling,
and Louis Tay, "Outcomes of Meaningful Work: A Meta Analysis,"
Journal of Management Studies, 56, no. 3 (May 2019): 500–528,
doi.org/10.1111/joms.12406.

134 *Michael Steger of Colorado State University said:* Joe Keohane,
"Everyone Wants Meaningful Work. But What Does That Look
Like, Really?" *Entrepreneur*, January 11, 2022, entrepreneur.com/
article/404066.

134 *In one Workhuman survey:* "Bringing More Humanity to
Recognition, Performance, and Life at Work—Workhuman
Research Institute: 2017 Survey Report," Workhuman, 2017,
workhuman.com/resources/papers/bringing-more-humanity-
to-recognition-performance-and-life-at-work.

134 *a report published by psychologists at the University of Toronto:*
Jing Hu and Jacob B. Hirsh, "Accepting Lower Salaries for
Meaningful Work," *Frontiers in Psychology*, September 29, 2017,
doi.org/10.3389/fpsyg.2017.01649.

136 *According to a YouGov poll:* Keohane, "Everyone Wants
Meaningful Work."

136 *A* Harvard Business Review *study found:* Shawn Achor,
Andrew Reece, Gabriella Rosen Kellerman, and Alexi Robichaux,
"9 Out of 10 People Are Willing to Earn Less Money to Do
More-Meaningful Work," *Harvard Business Review*, November 6,
2018, hbr.org/2018/11/9-out-of-10-people-are-willing-to-earn-less-
money-to-do-more-meaningful-work.

136 *As Deloitte found in one study: The 2016 Deloitte Millennial Survey:
Winning Over the Next Generation of Leaders*, Deloitte, 2016,
www2.deloitte.com/content/dam/Deloitte/global/Documents/
About-Deloitte/gx-millenial-survey-2016-exec-summary.pdf.

137 *exactly what happened on August 19, 2019:* "Statement on the
Purpose of a Corporation," Business Roundtable, letter, August 19,
2019, s3.amazonaws.com/brt.org/2022.06.01-BRTStatement
onthePurposeofaCorporationwithSignatures.pdf.

138 *They proclaimed a commitment to fostering:* "Business Roundtable
Redefines the Purpose of a Corporation to Promote 'An
Economy That Serves All Americans,'" Business Roundtable,
press release, August 19, 2019, businessroundtable.org/
business-roundtable-redefines-the-purpose-of-a-corporation-to-
promote-an-economy-that-serves-all-americans.

138 *Upon its release,* USA Today *called the statement:* Geoff Colvin, "America's Top CEOs Didn't Live Up to Their Promises in Business Roundtable Letter, Researchers Find," *Fortune,* August 5, 2021, fortune.com/2021/08/05/business-roundtable-letter-statement-on-the-purpose-of-a-corporation-stakeholder-capitalism-american-ceos/.

138 *two Harvard Business School professors have shown:* John Kotter and James L. Heskett, *Corporate Culture and Performance* (New York: Free Press, 1992).

138 *In one global study:* Afdhel Aziz, "Global Study Reveals Consumers Are Four to Six Times More Likely to Purchase, Protect and Champion Purpose-Driven Companies," *Forbes,* June 17, 2020, forbes.com/sites/afdhelaziz/2020/06/17/global-study-reveals-consumers-are-four-to-six-times-more-likely-to-purchase-protect-and-champion-purpose-driven-companies/?sh=c0eb6c6435fe.

139 *By 2025, Gen Z and millennial employees:* Anita Lettink, "No, Millennials Will NOT Be 75% of the Workforce in 2025 (or Ever)!" LinkedIn Pulse, September 17, 2019, linkedin.com/pulse/millennials-75-workforce-2025-ever-anita-lettink/.

139 *Deloitte found that workers under the age of forty: The Deloitte Global Millennial Survey 2019: Societal Discord and Technological Transformation Create a "Generation Disrupted,"* Deloitte, 2019, www2.deloitte.com/content/dam/Deloitte/global/Documents/About-Deloitte/deloitte-2019-millennial-survey.pdf.

139 *Another study found that 81 percent of these workers:* Ryan Rudominer, "Corporate Social Responsibility Matters: Ignore Millennials at Your Peril," *HuffPost,* February 5, 2016, huffingtonpost.com/ryan-rudominer/corporate-social-responsi_9_b_9155670.html.

139 *In yet a third study, 62 percent of millennials: 2015 Cone Communications Millennial CSR Study,* Cone, 2015, conecomm.com/2015-cone-communications-millennial-csr-study/.

139 *According to the 2022 Edelman Trust Barometer: 2022 Edelman Trust Barometer: The Cycle of Distrust,* Edelman, 2022, edelman.com/trust/2022-trust-barometer.

140 *When two researchers analyzed:* Lucian Bebchuk and Roberto Tallarita, "Have Business Roundtable Companies Lived Up to Their Stakeholder Commitments?" ProMarket, May 18, 2022, promarket.org/2022/05/18/business-roundtable-commitments-study-stakeholderism/.

144 *In a large study of more than four hundred US companies:*
Claudine Gartenberg, Andrea Prat, and George Serafeim,
"Corporate Purpose and Financial Performance," Harvard Business
School Working Paper, no. 17-023, September 2016,
dash.harvard.edu/handle/1/30903237?.

144 *just a 10 percent improvement in employees' connection:* Jake Herway,
"To Get Your People's Best Performance, Start with Purpose,"
Gallup, May 21, 2021, gallup.com/workplace/350060/
people-best-performance-start-purpose.aspx.

145 *A notable 37 percent of respondents:* Claire Hastwell,
"Creating a Culture of Recognition," Great Place to Work,
September 9, 2021, greatplacetowork.com/resources/blog/
creating-a-culture-of-recognition.

145 *In another report, 69 percent of employees:* Sabrina Son,
"12 Mind-Blowing Stats on Employee Recognition You Need
to Know," TINYpulse by Limeade, August 4, 2016,
https://www.tinypulse.com/blog/sk-employee-recognition-stats.

145 *recognition is a $46 billion a year industry:* Katie McCaskey,
"Employee Recognition Is a $46B Market Found in 2% of
Company Spending," eBallot, October 31, 2017, eballot.com/
blog/employee-recognition-is-a-46b-market-found-in-2-of-company-
spending.

145 *the most common type of recognition in the workplace:*
Son, "12 Mind-Blowing Stats."

146 *One study on motivation found that praise:* Martin Dewhurst,
Matthew Guthridge, and Elizabeth Mohr, "Motivating People:
Getting Beyond Money," *McKinsey Quarterly*, November 1, 2009,
mckinsey.com/business-functions/people-and-organizational-
performance/our-insights/motivating-people-getting-beyond-money.

147 *recognition has a "shelf life" of about one week:* Jennifer Robison,
"In Praise of Praising Your Employees," Gallup, November 9, 2006,
gallup.com/workplace/236951/praise-praising-employees.aspx.

147 *SHRM found that peer-to-peer recognition:* "Peer-to-Peer Is
35.7% More Likely to Have a Positive Impact on Financial
Results Than Manager-Only Recognition," SHRM/Globoforce
Employee Recognition Survey, 2012, slideshare.net/cakehr/
the-power-of-employee-appreciation-5-best-practices-in-employee-
recognition/36-Peertopeer_is_357_more_likely.

Chapter 9: Strengths

155 *Neuroscientists have shown:* Kendra Cherry, "What Is a State of Flow?" Verywell Mind, February 17, 2022, verywellmind.com/what-is-flow-2794768.

157 *In the most exhaustive literature review:* Marine Miglianico, Philippe Dubreuil, Paule Miquelon, Arnold B. Bakker, and Charles Martin-Krumm, "Strength Use in the Workplace: A Literature Review," *Journal of Happiness Studies* 21 (2020): 737–764, doi.org/10.1007/s10902-019-00095-w.

158 *Employees who are actively encouraged to use their strengths:* Miglianico et al., "Strength Use in the Workplace."

158 *Employees who get to use their strengths every day:* Brandon Rigoni and Jim Asplund, "Developing Employees' Strengths Boosts Sales, Profit, and Engagement," *Harvard Business Review*, September 1, 2016, hbr.org/2016/09/developing-employees-strengths-boosts-sales-profit-and-engagement.

158 *Gallup completed the most extensive study of workgroups:* Brandon Rigoni and Jim Asplund, "Strengths-Based Employee Development: The Business Results," Gallup, July 7, 2016, gallup.com/workplace/236297/strengths-based-employee-development-business-results.aspx.

163 *when strengths are recognized by close others:* S.L. Gable, C.L. Gosnell, N.C. Maisel, and A. Strachman, "Safely Testing the Alarm: Close Others' Responses to Personal Positive Events," *Journal of Personality and Social Psychology* 103, no. 6 (2012): 963–981, doi.org/10.1037/a0029488.

Chapter 10: Belonging

166 *According to a study from employee review site Glassdoor:* Jennifer Miller, "For Younger Job Seekers, Diversity and Inclusion in the Workplace Aren't a Preference. They're a Requirement," *Washington Post*, February 18, 2021, washingtonpost.com/business/2021/02/18/millennial-genz-workplace-diversity-equity-inclusion/.

166 *Another study by one of the world's largest consulting firms:* Heather Lawley, "Focusing on Diversity, Equity and Inclusion as Individual Concepts Is Key to Curbing the Great Resignation," Benefits PRO, February 11, 2022, benefitspro.com/2022/02/11/focusing-on-diversity-equity-and-inclusion-as-individual-concepts-is-key-to-curbing-the-great-resignation/?slreturn=20220208203608.

167   *ERGs are employee-led groups:* Claire Hastwell, "What Are Employee Resource Groups (ERGs)?" Great Place to Work, January 7, 2020, greatplacetowork.com/resources/blog/what-are-employee-resource-groups-ergs.

169   *Deloitte's researchers define "belonging" as:* Jeff Schwartz, David Mallon, Brad Denny, Yves Van Durme, Maren Hauptmann, Ramona Yan, and Shannon Poynton, "Belonging: From Comfort to Connection to Contribution," Deloitte Insights, May 15, 2020, www2.deloitte.com/us/en/insights/focus/human-capital-trends/2020/creating-a-culture-of-belonging.html.

169   *McKinsey found that a lack of belonging:* Aaron De Smet, Bonnie Dowling, Marino Mugayar-Baldocchi, and Bill Schaninger, "'Great Attrition' or 'Great Attraction'? The Choice Is Yours," September 8, 2021, *McKinsey Quarterly,* mckinsey.com/business-functions/people-and-organizational-performance/our-insights/great-attrition-or-great-attraction-the-choice-is-yours.

169   *As McKinsey put it:* Aaron De Smet, Bonnie Dowling, Marino Mugayar-Baldocchi, and Joe Spratt, "It's Not about the Office, It's about Belonging," *McKinsey Organization Blog,* January 13, 2022, mckinsey.com/business-functions/people-and-organizational-performance/our-insights/the-organization-blog/its-not-about-the-office-its-about-belonging.

169   *In a global study from Cognizant: What It Means to Belong @ Work,* Cognizant Reports, March 2020, cognizant.com/us/en/whitepapers/documents/what-it-means-to-belong-at-work-codex5471.pdf.

169   *Indeed's 2021 Work Happiness Score research:* Liz Lewis, "Workplace Well-Being Insights from the 2021 World Happiness Report," Indeed, March 20, 2021, indeed.com/lead/workplace-well-being-study-insights.

169   *just one incident of exclusion can lead to:* Evan W. Carr, Andrew Reece, Gabriella Rosen Kellerman, and Alexi Robichaux, "The Value of Belonging at Work," *Harvard Business Review,* December 16, 2019, hbr.org/2019/12/the-value-of-belonging-at-work.

170   *2022 Workplace Belonging Survey:* Mallory Newall and James Diamond, "Workers Agree, a Sense of Belonging at Work Boosts Productivity," Ipsos, January 24, 2022, ipsos.com/en-us/news-polls/belonging-boosts-productivity-Jan-2022.

170   *From a cost perspective, a focus on belonging:* Shirley J. Knowles, "Belonging: Your Cure for the Great Resignation," *Boston Business Journal*, November 30, 2021, bizjournals.com/boston/news/2021/11/30/belonging-your-cure-for-the-great-resignation.html.

170   *Dr. Rumeet Billan, who commissioned the Workplace Belonging Survey:* Newall and Diamond, "Workers Agree."

171   *organizations that establish this kind of culture are:* Schwartz et al., "Belonging."

175   *Research clearly shows that diverse teams:* David Rock and Heidi Grant, "Why Diverse Teams Are Smarter," *Harvard Business Review*, November 4, 2016, hbr.org/2016/11/why-diverse-teams-are-smarter.

175   *The Workplace Belonging Survey revealed that:* Rumeet Billan, "New Survey Reveals That Nearly Half of American Workers Are Considering Leaving Their Current Place of Employment," Cision PR Newswire, January 24, 2022, prnewswire.com/news-releases/new-survey-reveals-that-nearly-half-of-american-workers-are-considering-leaving-their-current-place-of-employment-301466289.html.

177   *Less than half (45 percent) of employed Americans:* Newall and Diamond, "Workers Agree."

177   *In a global survey of 31,000 workers:* Jared Spataro, "Great Expectations: A Road Map for Making Hybrid Work *Work*," Official Microsoft Blog, March 16, 2022, blogs.microsoft.com/blog/2022/03/16/great-expectations-a-roadmap-for-making-hybrid-work-work/.

180   *As Deloitte's researchers wrote regarding contributions:* Schwartz et al., "Belonging."

Chapter 11: Coaching

191   *study from Development Dimensions International:* Bruce Court, "Why Good Employees Leave and How to Retain Them," DDI, December 8, 2021, ddiworld.com/blog/why-good-employees-leave.

191   *In one survey of 14,500 US workers:* Zorana Ivcevic, Robin Stern, and Andrew Faas, "Research: What Do People Need to Perform at a High Level?" *Harvard Business Review*, May 17, 2021, hbr.org/2021/05/research-what-do-people-need-to-perform-at-a-high-level.

192   *Post-pandemic research by McKinsey found:* De Smet et al., "'Great Attrition' or 'Great Attraction'?"

194   *This is data compiled by Gallup:* Jim Clifton and Jim Harter, *It's The Manager: Moving from Boss to Coach* (New York: Gallup Press, 2019).

200   *These are the results that show up again and again:* Tonya Echols,
         "3 Key Coaching Skills for Leaders," Training Industry, December 6,
         2018, trainingindustry.com/articles/leadership/3-key-coaching-
         skills-for-leaders/.

200   *one meaningful coaching conversation each week:* Jim Clifton,
         "Gallup Finds a Silver Bullet: Coach Me Once per Week," Gallup,
         May 27, 2021, gallup.com/workplace/350057/gallup-finds-silver-
         bullet-coach-once-per-week.aspx.

200   *the Workplace Wellness Trends survey found: Workplace Wellness
         Trends: 2017 Survey Report*, International Foundation of Employee
         Benefit Plans, 2017, ifebp.org/bookstore/workplacewellness/Pages/
         default.aspx.

Chapter 12: Trust

204   *92 percent of people would trust their senior leader more if: The 2021
         Trust Outlook: Executive Edition*, Trust Edge Leadership Institute,
         2021, trustedge.com/wp-content/uploads/2021/06/2021-Trust-
         Outlook-Executive-Edition.pdf.

205   *only 40 percent of employees feel well informed:* Paul J. Zak,
         "The Neuroscience of Trust: Management Behaviors That Foster
         Employee Engagement," *Harvard Business Review*, January–February
         2017, hbr.org/2017/01/the-neuroscience-of-trust.

208   *remote workers are three times as likely to be engaged at work:*
         Adam Hickman and Jennifer Robison, "5 Facts about Engagement
         and Remote Workers," Gallup, May 1, 2020, gallup.com/
         workplace/309521/facts-engagement-remote-workers.aspx.

209   *where employees enjoy high amounts of trust:* Abbey Lewis,
         "Good Leadership? It All Starts with Trust," Harvard Business
         Publishing *Corporate Learning* blog, October 26, 2022,
         harvardbusiness.org/good-leadership-it-all-starts-with-trust/.

209   *Trust has a major impact on employee loyalty:* Zak, "The Neuroscience
         of Trust."

209   *59 percent of employees said:* "Survey: More Than Half of Employees
         Have Worked for a Micromanager," Cision PR Newswire,
         July 1, 2014, prnewswire.com/news-releases/survey-more-than-half-
         of-employees-have-worked-for-a-micromanager-265359491.html.

209   *Micromanaging includes tracking:* Mita Mallick, "4 Ways to Be a
         Better Boss during 'the Great Resignation,'" *Fast Company*, August
         20, 2021, fastcompany.com/90667628/4-ways-to-be-a-better-boss-
         during-the-great-resignation.

213   *A Citigroup and LinkedIn survey found:* Rachel Feintzeig, "Flexibility at Work: Worth Skipping a Raise?" *Washington Post*, October 31, 2014, wsj.com/articles/BL-ATWORKB-2141.

Chapter 13: Advocacy

222   *instead treats them with respect:* Emma Seppälä, "Why Compassion Is a Better Managerial Tactic Than Toughness," *Harvard Business Review*, May 7, 2015, hbr.org/2015/05/why-compassion-is-a-better-managerial-tactic-than-toughness.

224   *story of Jim, an IT Developer:* u/vbigoof, "'Twas the Night before My Resignation..." Reddit, January 3, 2022, reddit.com/r/RegularRevenge/comments/rvghty/twas_the_night_before_my_resignation/.

230   *McKinsey surveyed more than fifty thousand supervisors: Leadership Capacity: The New Science of Breathing Life into Your Teams,* CultureSmith Inc., 2020, f.hubspotusercontent40.net/hubfs/7685092/Marketing%20Documents/eBooks/Leadership%20Capacity%20ebook.pdf.

Chapter 14: Starting an Employalty Movement in Your Organization

241   *In one study on effective managers:* Clifton and Harter, *It's the Manager.*

248   *My favorite definition of the word "culture":* Terrence E. Deal and Allan A. Kennedy, *Corporate Cultures: The Rites and Rituals of Corporate Life* (Reading, MA: Addison-Wesley Publishing Company, 1982), 126.

Chapter 15: The Blockbuster Epilogue

252   *In his book* That Will Never Work*:* Marc Randolph, *That Will Never Work: The Birth of Netflix and the Amazing Life of an Idea* (New York: Little, Brown, 2019).

254   *The media giant went from having:* "Blockbuster LLC Company History Timeline," Zippia, zippia.com/blockbuster-llc-careers-1327661/history/.

About the Author

JOE MULL has spent nearly two decades teaching leaders how to be better bosses and make work *work* for all. In demand as a keynote speaker, Joe is the host of the popular *Boss Better Now* podcast and founder of the BossBetter Leadership Academy. He is the author of three books, previously managed training at one of the largest healthcare systems in the US, and appears regularly as a leadership and retention expert in the media. Joe resides near Pittsburgh, PA, with his wife, three children, and a needy Dalmatian named Flash.

ARE YOU PLANNING A MEETING, CONFERENCE, OR EVENT?

Invite Joe Mull to be your keynote speaker

"We never imagined it was possible to have such an engaging program. Joe Mull exceeded every expectation. He is an *amazing* speaker. Our attendees loved his program. He actually gave me goosebumps."

STEPHANIE HANEY, Blue Cross Blue Shield

For more information, visit **joemull.com** or email **hello@joemull.com**